AUS TRA LIA

Travel with Marco Polo Insider Tips

INSIDER TIP
Your shortcut to a great experience

T0001627

MARCO POLO
TOP HIGHLIGHTS

BLUE MOUNTAINS NATIONAL PARK ⭐
Endless forests, steep gorges and sacred Aboriginal sites: welcome to the wilderness on Sydney's doorstep.

➤ p. 52, Sydney

KAKADU NATIONAL PARK ⭐
The continent's tropical north offers rock paintings, crocodiles and fascinating nature.

➤ p. 114, Northern Territory

GREAT BARRIER REEF ⭐
Off the coast of Queensland, the reef is a must for divers, sailors and nature lovers.
📷 *Tip: No pricey underwater cameras needed on Lady Elliot Island. The reef starts at the beach!*

➤ p. 86, Queensland

OPERA HOUSE ⭐
The shell-shaped building on Sydney Harbour is an architectural masterpiece – and a Down Under landmark.
📷 *Tip: The northern tip of the Domain (near Mrs Macquaire's Chair) offers incredible views of the Opera House.*

➤ p. 43, Sydney

ULURU-KATA TJUTA NATIONAL PARK 5
These days you can't climb it, but imposing Uluru (formerly Ayers Rock) remains a must-see.

➤ p. 119, Northern Territory

BAROSSA VALLEY ⭐
Wine, rye bread and smoked ham – plus historic villages with beautiful scenery.

➤ p. 149, South Australia

KANGAROO ISLAND

The wilderness hides penguins, mysterious sea dragons, rare kangaroos, koalas and huge seal colonies.

📷 *Tip: Follow the boardwalk at Admirals Arch to the end. Seals almost always play on the cliffs here.*

➤ p. 148, South Australia

CRADLE MOUNTAIN-LAKE ST CLAIR NATIONAL PARK

Immerse yourself in Tasmania's untamed landscape: rugged mountain giants, still lakes deeper than you could imagine, swamps and moss-covered primeval forests.

➤ p. 164, Tasmania

GREAT OCEAN ROAD

One of the world's most stunning coastal roads, with bizarre rock formations, impressive cliffs (photo), wonderful views and mysterious forests.

📷 *Tip: Walk down Gibson Steps near the Twelve Apostles. At low tide, you'll come face to face with the rocks.*

➤ p. 166, Discovery Tours

FRASER ISLAND (K'GARI)

The world's largest sand island offers endless beaches, with dingoes on land and whales and dolphins offshore.

📷 *Tip: Boat tours between August and October are the perfect opportunity to spot a humpback whale.*

➤ p. 94, Queensland

CONTENTS

NORTHERN TERRITORY

WESTERN AUSTRALIA

QUEENSLAND

SOUTH AUSTRALIA

SYDNEY

NEW SOUTH WALES

VICTORIA

TASMANIA

36   REGIONAL OVERVIEW

38   SYDNEY
52 Around Sydney

54   NEW SOUTH WALES
58 Byron Bay 59 Port Macquarie
61 Batemans Bay 63 Canberra
66 Broken Hill

70   VICTORIA
74 Melbourne 83 Grampians

86   QUEENSLAND
90 Brisbane 95 Airlie Beach
98 Townsville 99 Cairns

106 NORTHERN TERRITORY
110 Darwin
114 Kakadu National Park
116 Katherine 117 Alice Springs

122 WESTERN AUSTRALIA
126 Perth 129 Margaret River
132 Exmouth 134 Broome
137 Kimberley 138 Kununurra

140 SOUTH AUSTRALIA
144 Adelaide 152 Coober Pedy

154   TASMANIA
158 Hobart 160 Launceston
162 St Helens 163 Devonport
164 Cradle Mountain-Lake
St Clair National Park 165 Strahan

CONTENTS

MARCO POLO TOP HIGHLIGHTS
2   Top ten highlights

BEST OF AUSTRALIA
8   ... when it rains
9   ... on a budget
10   ... with children
11   ... classic experiences

GET TO KNOW AUSTRALIA
14   Discover Australia
17   At a glance
18   Understand Australia
21   True or false?

EATING, SHOPPING, SPORT
26   Eating & drinking
30   Shopping
32   Sport & activities

MARCO POLO REGIONS

36   Regional overview

DISCOVERY TOURS

166 Spectacular coastal trip: Great
     Ocean Road
171 A journey through dreamtime
174 Rainforest hike in Lamington
     National Park

GOOD TO KNOW

176 **HOLIDAY BASICS**
     *Arrival, Getting around, Festivals
     & events, Emergencies,
     Essentials, Weather*

186 **HOLIDAY VIBES**
     Books, films, music & blogs

188 **TRAVEL PURSUIT**
     The Marco Polo holiday quiz

190 **INDEX & CREDITS**

☉ Plan your visit
$–$$$ Price categories
(*) Premium-rate
     phone number

🍴 Eating/drinking
🛍 Shopping
🍸 Nightlife
🏖 Top beaches

☂ Rainy day activities
🐷 Budget activities
👪 Family activities
🚩 Classic experiences

(▣ A2) Refers to removable pull-out map
(0) Located off the map

BEST OF AUSTRALIA

The view of Uluru at sunset is hard to beat

BEST ☂ WHEN IT RAINS

ACTIVITIES TO BRIGHTEN YOUR DAY

GIANT KANGAROOS & ANCIENT LIZARDS

The extensive collections in the *Australian Museum* provide a fascinating insight into the natural history of the ancient continent.

➤ p. 46, Sydney

TALES OF IMMIGRANTS

Discover how early immigrants to Australia made their way across the seas – often packed into cramped quarters below deck – at the *Immigration Museum* in Melbourne.

➤ p. 74, Victoria

SHOP TILL YOU DROP

Some 180 shops and countless restaurants and snack bars fill the *Melbourne Central* shopping centre (photo). You can easily spend hours here (window) shopping.

➤ p. 80, Victoria

EXPLORE THE REEF

Let the weather gods rage all they like – in the parallel universe of the *Great Barrier Reef*, it's business as usual. Dives are only cancelled when hurricane warnings are issued.

➤ p. 96, Queensland

ROCK IN THE RAIN

An unusual natural wonder is not to be missed at *Uluru (Ayers Rock)* when it pours with rain. Torrents flow down the smooth sides of the monolith, waterfalls plunge from far above and fountains shoot out of openings in the rock.

➤ p. 119, Northern Territory

VALUABLE ART OR WHAT?

Outside Hobart, the *Mona (Museum of Old and New Art)* is an art experience of a special kind: for example, a single machine fills an entire room, and it's a machine that converts food into excrement.

➤ p. 158, Tasmania

BEST ON A BUDGET

FOR SMALLER WALLETS

PATIENT PATIENTS

In the *Koala Hospital*, a large animal clinic run by volunteers in Port Macquarie, ailing koalas are nursed back to good health and returned to the wild. The best time to visit is 3pm when the cuddly marsupials are fed (a small donation is required).

➤ p. 60, New South Wales

ART FOR ART'S SAKE

Admission to Australia's biggest art gallery, the *National Gallery of Australia*, in Canberra's government district won't cost you a cent. Just be sure to allow plenty of time, because there are over 160,000 works by Australian and international artists.

➤ p.64, New South Wales

FREE TRANSPORT

No tickets are needed for the *City Circle Tram* (photo) that travels around Melbourne's city centre. Many sights can easily be reached on foot from the tram stops.

➤ p. 74, Victoria

SWIM IN THE CITY

As the tropical town of Cairns doesn't have a decent sandy beach, a generously sized recreational oasis has been created between the pedestrian precinct and the coastal promenade with saltwater pools, a sunbathing area and barbecues. The *Esplanade Swimming Lagoon* is a popular meeting place – not least because it's free.

➤ p. 101, Queensland

ADELAIDE GREETERS

The friendly folk who welcome visitors to their city are know as the Adelaide Greeters. The free service is provided by volunteers and is currently offered in Sydney, Melbourne, Brisbane and Cairns, as well as Adelaide.

➤ p.144, South Australia

BEST WITH CHILDREN

FUN FOR YOUNG & OLD

CHILD'S PLAY

Take the kids to one of Australia's many impressive playgrounds and they're sure to be talking about it for years to come. At the water-based *children's playground* at Darling Harbour, for example, everyone – big and small alike – will get their money's worth. Just make sure to pack a change of clothes!
➤ p.47, Sydney

MAKING LEARNING FUN

The *Questacon* in Canberra is full of irresistible experiments. Who hasn't dreamed of playing air hockey against a robot, experiencing a simulated earthquake or triggering a tsunami?
➤ p. 65, New South Wales

FARMER FOR THE DAY

Collingwood Children's Farm in Melbourne brings country living to the city. Kids can pet the goats and sheep, ride ponies and watch the cows being milked.
➤ p. 79, Victoria

CROCODILE ALERT

On a *boat ride along the Adelaide River*, you can watch saltwater crocodiles leap gracefully out of the water for the bait that is held over the railing. An unforgettable experience!
➤ p. 112, Northern Territory

UP CLOSE & PERSONAL WITH KANGAROOS

Of course, you can see kangaroos, koalas and emus in the wild in Australia, but you need a certain amount of luck and patience to do so. At the *Cleland Wildlife Park* in Adelaide, the animals live in a natural bush environment and you can even feed them.
➤ p. 146, South Australia

BEST
CLASSIC EXPERIENCES

ONLY IN AUSTRALIA

GLAMPING WITH WALLABIES & WOMBATS

The wind is howling around the tent, and somewhere a wombat is scrabbling about – it's really cosy even though you're in the middle of the bush at *Wilderness Retreats* in Victoria's Wilsons Promontory National Park.
➤ p. 85, Victoria

CREATURE COMFORTS

The *Koala Sanctuary* is the largest koala animal park in the world, as well as being home to other native animals. On the outskirts of Brisbane you can come face to face with platypuses, gawky flightless birds, tame kangaroos and other marsupials.
➤ p. 91, Queensland

A TASTE OF AUSTRALIA

The innovative menu served in the popular *Ochre Restaurant* in Cairns prides itself on showcasing Australian ingredients: crocodile, kangaroo or emu meat, local berries and bush tomatoes.
➤ p. 101, Queensland

EXPERIENCE LOCAL CULTURE

Cook damper (unleavened bread), dig through the mud for water caltrop (water chestnuts) and discover what ants taste like. On the *Animal Tracks Safari*, visitors spend a day exploring the far-flung corners of the *Kakadu National Park* and learning about the area's millennia-old indigenous food traditions with a local guide.
➤ p. 114, Northern Territory

FRUIT OF THE AUSTRALIAN EARTH

Many wineries offer wine tasting (photo) – usually free of charge. Your best option is to join a tour for your visit. But remember: the blood-alcohol driving limit is 0.5 per cent!
➤ p. 150, South Australia

GET TO KNOW AUSTRALIA

The outback at sunset: a mob of kangaroos gather to feed

DISCOVER AUSTRALIA

The sweeping lines of Elizabeth Quay Bridge join Perth City to the waterfront

Everyone is familiar with the Sydney Opera House, Uluru (Ayers Rock), boomerangs and kangaroos. And everyone knows that the spiders are poisonous, that koalas sleep a lot and that Australians are pretty laid-back. But, let's be honest, many visitors from the Northern Hemisphere don't know a whole lot more about the vast red continent on the other side of the planet.

THE UNKNOWN SOUTH

Historically, it's not that long since people in Europe first became aware of Australia. Until Captain James Cook's return from his first South Sea voyage in 1771, existence of the "Terra Australis Incognita" – the unknown land in the south – was just a suspicion. Imagine it: the machine age had begun in Europe, and astronomers knew how to calculate the exact distance between the Sun and the

70,000–64,000 BCE
Aboriginal people settle Australia

1770
Captain James Cook claims the continent for the British Crown

1788
Great Britain uses Australia as a penal colony

1851
Gold is discovered, drawing people from across the globe

1901
The colonies unite to form a federation

1905–1970
Aboriginal Australian children are taken from their families – history's *stolen*

Earth, but somehow we had completely overlooked the existence of the world's biggest island, an earth mass more than 35 times the size of Great Britain.

And what a bizarre world it was: the trees shed their bark instead of their leaves. Swans were black, not white. The seasons were the wrong way round. And the naturalists could not find any words for the newly discovered creatures, let alone allocate them to any of the existing categories. "It is not possible to compare it to a European animal because it does not bear the slightest resemblance to any I know," was how Joseph Banks, a man not otherwise known to be lost for words, tried to describe a kangaroo. Little wonder, then, that these brief descriptions captured the imagination and created such a stir. It was to be many, many years before naturalists began to fill in the gaps in their knowledge. The fascination remains to this day.

LAND OF THE DREAMTIME

Although Europeans still consider Australia to be a young country, to Aboriginal Australians it is anything but. Australia's First Peoples had inhabited the continent for at least 60,000 years by the time Captain Cook set anchor here. This makes Australian Aboriginal culture the oldest continuously existing culture in human history. But that's not all: Aboriginal beliefs, ways of life and spirituality are so enduring that, even today, Indigenous Australians are able to interpret the messages handed down by their ancestors in their rock paintings or verses

generation

1942
Japanese bombers attack Darwin. Australian soldiers fight on the side of the Allies

2008
Prime Minister Kevin Rudd issues an apology to the victims of the *stolen generation*

2015
Parliament passes "The Reef 2050 Plan" to protect the Great Barrier Reef

2019
The Australian Bramble Cay mosaic-tailed rat is officially declared extinct, making it the first mammal to fall victim to climate change

with the same ease as they would, perhaps, an SMS from a modern-day cousin. A deep affinity for their land has resulted in a lifestyle that has stood in a perfect balance with nature for thousands of years.

In Aboriginal Australian mythology, every single person is a direct descendant of an ancestral being in the story of their creation. This phase, called the dreamtime, is handed down in paintings and songs. However, a person is only initiated into the knowledge to which they are entitled on the basis of their gender, age and ranking. Uninitiated outsiders are only given brief insights into a very small part of Indigenous Australian mythology.

TWO WORLDS COLLIDE
The Aboriginal peoples of Australia see it as their role to look after the land and all living beings on it, and to preserve the natural balance. The idea of ownership, of possession, brought in by the white settlers was as strange to Australia's indigenous populations as farming or the building of permanent settlements. Whites, in turn, made a fatal assumption when they saw the lack of solid buildings and the absence of any obvious cultivation of the land: in the Proclamation of Terra Nullius, they declared Australia to be a no man's land. The subsequent seizure of land caused the destruction of natural habitats and sparked brutal confrontations between the indigenous people and the new arrivals. The diseases the settlers brought with them did even more harm. In many areas, local indigenous populations were virtually wiped out within a very short time. The fiction of Terra Nullius was not repealed until 1992, and coexistence of Aboriginal and settler cultures remains a contentious and emotive topic in Australia to this day, with many open wounds.

DIFFERENT COUNTRIES, DIFFERENT YARDSTICKS
By land, it's about 4,000km from Sydney on the east coast to Perth in the west. Travel from Adelaide in the south to Darwin in the tropical north, and you'll find yourself clocking up at least 3,000km. The continent's almost 7.7 million km² is home to just over 25 million people. These are the sort of benchmark figures you need to keep in mind when planning your trip.

So what appeals to you about Australia? Is it the charm of the cosmopolitan centres such as Sydney and Melbourne? Or the endless deserted sandy beaches or the Great Barrier Reef? Are you looking for the perfect wave? Or are you drawn to the world of the Outback? Whichever destinations you choose, leave time and space for spontaneous exploration, for surprising encounters and for sunsets that are still fascinating long after the glowing sphere has disappeared beyond the horizon. Because these are the experiences that you will never forget.

INSIDER TIP
Less is more

AT A GLANCE

25,500,000
inhabitants

Sydney: 5,370,000
London: 8,800,000

35,877km
Coastline

**Longest beach:
Ninety Mile Beach**

151km
In the UK:
Chesil Beach: 29km

7,692,000km^2
Area

Sydney: 12,368km^2
UK: 243,610km^2

LONGEST STRAIGHT RAILWAY LINE IN THE WORLD

478km
through the Nullarbor Plain

POPULATION BORN OUTSIDE AUSTRALIA

28.2%

MOST POPULAR TIMES TO VISIT SYDNEY

September–November
and
March–May

19 UNESCO WORLD HERITAGE SITES

including the Great Barrier Reef, Daintree Rainforest, Fraser Island, Sydney Opera House

MOUNT KOSCIUSZKO

is the tallest mountain at 2,228m

Ben Nevis: 1,344m

DAYS OF SUNSHINE IN SYDNEY

107
per year

UNDERSTAND AUSTRALIA

BULADJANG, OR THE REVENGE OF URANIUM

In the tropical north of Australia is a region that has been taboo to the local Aboriginal people for thousands of years. *Buladjang* – which means "Sickness Country" – is what they call this mystical region close to Kakadu National Park. According to the traditional Aboriginal story of creation, this is where the ancestral Bula spirit created the landscape as he walked and hunted: marshes, savannah woodlands and rocks. When he had finished his work, Bula went underground to rest, and must not be disturbed as he can cause all kinds of natural disasters.

The Aboriginal people have known for thousands of years that the water here is toxic, and that eating anything that grows here causes disease. The white prospectors who burst on the scene at the beginning of the 20th century and called the saltwater crocodiles "alligators" and described the local people as "primitive", thought this was all most suspicious. Without wasting too much time on international basic principles or niceties such as respect, they forced their way into the forbidden zone – and found the richest uranium ore deposits on the planet.

You might now ask yourself what this story has to do with Australia today. It's easy: it is a typical, often-repeated example of the crass clash between two world views that could not be more different from each other, and whose collateral damage continues to the present.

It is possibly one of the most unfortunate ironies in the history of mankind that an ancient people, whose existence has only left the faintest traces on Mother Earth, even after thousands of years, should be the custodian of a mineral that not only gave rise to a new industrial revolution in the Western world, but also led to the development of various devastating weapons of mass destruction. The interaction between Indigenous and incoming people and the coexistence of their cultures remain extremely sensitive issues to this day.

GREY NOMADS

The Aussies love camping. It's a tradition: even the pioneers moved around the country with a *swag*, a voluminous sleeping bag. To this day, Australians like to pack up all their gear at the weekend and build a temporary home out of canvas and tent poles somewhere in the wilderness. During school holidays, expect to compete with hordes of Australian families for space on the campsite. Oh, and then, of course, there are the "grey nomads", for whom camping is both a leisure activity and a philosophy of life. These are pensioners who love travelling, and often swap their homes for a caravan or mobile home to travel the continent in tune with the seasons. By the way, these mature globe-trotters

Get used to sharing your campsite with the local wildlife

are an inexhaustible source of insider tips for travellers.

CREEPY CRAWLIES

Of all the strange creatures in the Australian animal world, ranging from cute to scary, visitors probably pay the most attention to its spiders. Just how dangerous are they? In fact, there are a number of spiders whose poison can be fatal for humans. They include Sydney's funnel-web spider and the harmless-looking redback spider, which is found all over Australia. The good news is that, with the introduction of antidotes in the early 1980s, the number of deaths from spider bites dropped to zero. However, it is important that you seek medical assistance promptly if you are bitten. Be particularly careful on walkabouts in the bush. Walking face-first into a vast, thickly spun spider's web is about as creepy as suddenly having a parachute thrown over you – just slightly less pleasant.

DON'T ADAPT TOO MUCH!

Almost half of all Australians either emigrated here themselves or had at least one parent who did. But multiculturalism, far from being hype in Australia, is the government's official creed. Immigrants are encouraged to preserve their cultural and linguistic singularities, because they are the core of the national identity. New arrivals never have a strange culture forced upon them, but are asked what they bring with them that will enrich Australia. Can this work? Decide for yourself in multicultural Melbourne.

The fantastical duck-billed platypus puzzled naturalists for decades

Incidentally, Australia plans to double its current population of 25 million through immigration by 2050. However, the authorities are extremely selective in their choice of candidates, and the immigration criteria became much stricter in 2017. What the effects of this political realignment in terms of immigration policy are on society remains to be seen.

BEASTLY FUN

"Bears" that spend the day sleeping in the branches of trees. Marsupials that leap across the ground as if on springs. Coin-sized insects with a poisonous bite that can fell a horse. The Creator must have been in a funny mood when he focused his attention on Australia's animal world. Can you imagine what the early settlers must have thought of all this?

Here is just one example: the *platypus* posed quite a conundrum for the first naturalists "down under". In fact, those who had never seen one in the wild thought this curious creature was so odd that it could only be a fake – a joke by a clever taxidermist. It rather resembled a flattened beaver with a duck's beak. However, its reproductive habits were even more curious than its external appearance. Ninety years passed before a Scottish biologist finally managed to slay an unfortunate female with an unlaid egg in her womb. This was the first evidence of the existence of an egg-laying mammal – also referred to, somewhat unfortunately, as monotremes. Once again, Australia had turned the organised world of the Europeans upside down.

Today, climate change is taking its toll on Australian wildlife. The Bramble

Cay mosaic-tailed rat, found solely on the small island of the same name just north of the Great Barrier Reef, went down in history as the first mammal to be driven to extinction by climate change.

GREEN MOVEMENTS ON THE RED CONTINENT

When it comes to environmentalism, the contrasts in Australia are at least as marked as in the environment itself. The first settlers demonstrated little restraint in the way they used and treated nature. It's not hard to see why: most of them were convicts who had been sent here against their will. Their only aim was to create a tolerable existence for themselves in this unforgiving landscape. But the trees continued to fall long after the initial need for survival. Diggers continue

TRUE OR FALSE?

IT'S ALL DUST & DESERT

OK, granted, the numbers do little to disprove the old cliché: 70 per cent of the Australian continent is either arid or semi-arid – in other words, it's dry. But Australians tend to settle somewhere else entirely, with over 80 per cent of the population living less than 100km from the coast. For the most part, urban Australia is as modern, futuristic even, as Manhattan or Dubai. So if you're dreaming of an adventure that's a little more *Crocodile Dundee*, you'll need to head for the Outback.

AUSSIES LOVE A FOSTER'S

Well, maybe a few … on holiday in Europe, where the largest-selling Australian beer brand makes the most of its "down under" connotations. But at home Australians prefer a glass (or two) of Carlton Draught, XXXX or Victoria Bitter. Australians are also increasingly enjoying craft beers from the countless microbreweries scattered across the country. Why not try a Balter XPA, Fat Yak or 4 Pines when you get the chance?

their search for profitable natural resources to this day, even in protected areas. This is something even the first environmental activists, who organised themselves politically here before any other country in the world, were unable to change.

The Australians are also experiencing the full force of the consequences of climate change: hurricanes and continuing storms repeatedly destroy and flood large areas of Queensland, while further south there is the fear of devastating forest fires during the long, hot droughts. But the attitude of society as a whole is gradually changing now that the Great Barrier Reef is experiencing the worst episode of coral bleaching in its history (see p. 97).

TYPICAL AUSSIE

One nice characteristic from the pioneering era has managed to survive to this day – the seemingly boundless helpfulness of the Australians, regardless of whether you have a puncture in the outback or have lost your way in Sydney or Melbourne. Appointments are rescheduled just to get you back on the road, maps are organised, routes explained – and all with a patience and friendliness that make most Europeans gasp in amazement. At such moments you really experience how strong the bond between Australians actually is, and that the solidarity they feel for one another is one of the nation's fundamental values.

Australians react very sensitively to arrogance and presumptuousness.

Tall poppy syndrome is what they call it when celebrities claim too much of the limelight – either through a nervous gaggle of bodyguards or, as in the case of politicians, through too great a distance to the man on the street. Tall poppies, many people think, have to be brought back down to earth again.

GOD SAVE THE KING

The British monarch, King Charles III, is Australia's Head of State. He appoints a Governor General as his representative as suggested by the Australian government. And this representative in turn gives his or her blessing to the ministers who are suggested by the Prime Minister. Do you think all that's rather complicated and outdated? A referendum in 1999 surprisingly confirmed that Australians would rather remain loyal to the Crown than become a republic. Nonetheless, republican noises are still being made from time to time, and it is not beyond the realms of possibility that Australia may well question its position as a federal parliamentary constitutional monarchy before much longer with another referendum.

THE RACE THAT STOPS THE NATION

If you happen to be travelling unsuspectingly on a bus in Australia at just before 3pm on the first Tuesday in November, don't be surprised if the driver suddenly pulls over, pulls on the brake and without further ado disappears into the pub on the corner of the street; or if you're in the supermarket, you may find that the checkout remains unmanned for several minutes. The street may suddenly completely empty – where is everybody? It's Melbourne Cup Day! And there's a good reason why Australia's most prestigious horse race is known as "the race that stops the nation".

No other day in the year unites the Australian nation like this one: the day on which the country stops – to collectively watch the horse they've backed. About 80 per cent of the adult Australian population put their money on at least one horse, which means the Cup has long since grown beyond the borders of true racing fans. It's just part of the charm of this event that many an ambitious speculator who has spent months studying the form and performance of the horses ends up shredding their betting slips in sheer frustration, while the slightly tipsy lady standing close by is amused by the fact that she only chose the one that went on to win because she could still say its name after consuming two bottles of champagne. Melbourne Cup Day is even an official public holiday in the state of Victoria.

FLYING DOCTORS

The first medical emergency service by air in the world began in 1928 as the Australian Aerial Medical Service in the small town of Cloncurry in Queensland, after the Presbyterian pastor John Flynn had seen the misery of those living in the outback for himself. Being so far from medical help, many people died as the result of injuries and illnesses that would have been treated easily in towns. Today, the Royal Flying Doctor Service (RFDS) operates from 21 bases, from which they serve an area of 7.3 million km², roughly 30 times the size of the United Kingdom.

The Flying Doctors deal with medical cases – from births to accidents – in the outback

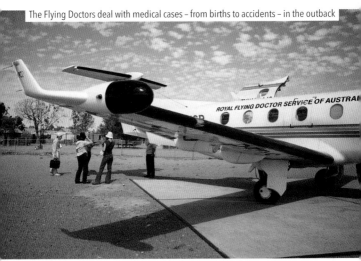

EATING
SHOPPING
SPORT

Melbourne has a diverse and dynamic restaurant scene

EATING & DRINKING

Try barramundi cooked in paper-bark, Moroccan-spiced kangaroo tenderloin or pizza topped with crocodile meat, and add to that a craft beer or glass of Sauvignon Blanc from the local winery. Australia is a paradise for lovers of fresh, light and varied food.

ONCE A GOURMET DESERT ...

Back in the late 1990s, Australia's culinary culture still left a bad taste (sometimes literally) in the mouth of the country's gourmets. The restaurant on the corner offered the same over-cooked steak and limp vegetables as the pub across the street. Bread came in a plastic bag, and it didn't take much to leave it compacted to just an inch or so thick. Beer was only available from industrial breweries that seemed to value quantity over quality.

... NOW A CULINARY MELTING POT

Thankfully, that's a thing of the past. Actually, it's better than that. Today, Australia offers a wealth of culinary experiences that even a local would struggle to get through.

Australia has the many immigrants from across the globe to thank for that. Over the past few decades, they have made the country their home, responding to the poor food on offer with a mix of homesickness and inspiration. First, whole neighbourhoods sprung up devoted entirely to Italian or Chinese cuisine, for example. New cuisines quickly joined the pot, and now you can find *yum cha* next to the fish & chip shop, while further down the street fresh falafels are frying and Vietnamese *pho* is bubbling away.

Grilled red mullet with coleslaw (left); pavlova (right)

FUSION FOOD

Today you'll find specialities from Spain to Shanghai and Siberia to Samoa not just on the same street, but also often on the same plate.

DER TIP
Multicultural menus

How about, for example, pork belly with oyster sauce? French scallops with Vietnamese coleslaw? Welcome to fusion food, the trend that brings together the most diverse culinary cultures and arts in a single dish. And there's nowhere better to sample the success of these blends than Melbourne or Sydney.

MARKET DAY

No trip is complete without a visit to one of the old markets, such as Central Market in Adelaide or the Queen Victoria Market in Melbourne. You'll find a stunning variety of fresh salads, exotic vegetables and tasty fruit. And most of it is grown in Australia – juicy fragrant mangos, sweet pineapples, bananas and coconuts from the tropical north; aromatic peaches, passionfruit, melons, lychees and citrus fruit from Victoria and New South Wales; and apples and pears from Tasmania. On top of this, there are numerous Asian leafy vegetables, tender broccolini, avocados, sweet potatoes and a huge selection of fresh herbs and spices.

Meat comes from cattle and sheep raised naturally on open pastureland – and from kangaroos, emus and crocodiles. The large fish markets stock everything the ocean, rivers and lakes have to offer, such as tender white barramundi from the saltwaters of the north, John Dory from the bottom of the ocean, excellent fresh tuna, tangerine-coloured salmon, and delicious giant crabs, oysters and other shellfish.

example, or roasting kangaroo on charcoal and using spices and ingredients, such as water caltrop, foraged from the wild.

BOUTIQUE BEER & FINE WINE

A pint of draught beer from one of the big breweries might lack something of the taste and zest of European beers. However, the same cannot be said about the often excellent beer produced by the various small boutique breweries.

Australian wines are excellent: earthy dry reds and refreshing whites – these are world class. German and Italian immigrants took the first proper vines with them to Australia and, today, Australian wine is exported around the globe.

COFFEE AT ITS BEST

Aussies love a good cup of coffee, especially in the big cities. This is thanks to Italian immigrants who, from the early days, started importing their highly polished espresso machines from home. In the meantime, the Aussies have developed a coffee culture of their very own. If you order a short black, you'll get a plain espresso; a long black is two-thirds water and one-third espresso. Extremely popular – and something of an invention from Australia/New Zealand – is the flat white: two shots of espresso topped up with steamed milk and finished with a layer of microfoam, not to be confused with a latte (milk coffee) or a cappuccino.

A favourite with those in the know: wine from the Barossa Valley

ABORIGINAL FOOD

For a long time, the culinary culture of Aboriginal Australians was regarded as totally incompatible with European eating habits, not least because it is based on the consumption of only those ingredients that the great outdoors makes available at any time. Agriculture and food preservation, therefore, are not part of the tradition.

Now, some restaurants are trying to revive indigenous cuisines, cooking barramundi in paperbark, for

TODAY'S SPECIALS

Starters

BARBECUED PRAWNS
Marinated barbecued giant prawns

CRAB SALAD
Cooked crab on a bed of fresh salad

GARLIC BREAD
Fresh sourdough with garlic butter

Mains

BARRAMUNDI FILLETS WITH MACADAMIA NUTS
Breaded barramundi with chopped macadamia nuts, served with salad

KANGAROO BURGER WITH BEETROOT
Kangaroo patty in a burger bun with beetroot

LEG OF LAMB WITH ROASTED VEGGIES
Oven-roasted leg of lamb seasoned with garlic, rosemary and honey, served with vegetables

CROCODILE PIZZA
With optional added kangaroo or emu meat

Desserts

PAVLOVA
Meringue with fresh cream, berries, peaches, kiwis and passion fruit

LAMINGTON
Soft sponge cake dipped in chocolate and sprinkled with coconut flakes

ANZAC BISCUIT
Oat biscuit with sugar beet syrup

TIM TAM
Australia's favourite chocolate biscuit

Drinks

CRAFT BEER
Beer from an independent brewery

SAUVIGNON BLANC
From the Hunter Valley

SHIRAZ
From the Barossa Valley

FLAT WHITE
Espresso with hot milk

SHOPPING

DREAMTIME SOUVENIRS

You don't have to go far in Australian cities or tourist hotspots to find boomerangs, clap sticks or didgeridoos. Everywhere you look, there are souvenir shops selling Aboriginal handicrafts. But watch out: all too often, these are mass-produced articles that no Aboriginal Australian ever had anything to do with. But as a lay person, how can you tell the difference between genuinely hand-made crafts and copies? You can rely on certified Aboriginal art galleries, cultural centres and community art centres. And check the label of authenticity, as it should have a registration number indicating the artist who made the item. Small workshops in the outback often offer the most authentic souvenirs.

INSIDER TIP
How to avoid fakes

PRECIOUS STONES & PEARLS

Near Broome in the north of Western Australia, elegant, cultured pearls are farmed in the coastal waters; whereas valuable sapphires and opals are dug from the earth in the interior of the continent. The best prices are to be obtained locally, e.g. opals in Coober Pedy (South Australia) and Lightning Ridge (New South Wales), and sapphires in the Central Highlands (Queensland). The jewellery shops in the major cities work against this by offering fancy settings. Alternatively, you could buy an uncut stone or a pearl without a setting and have your gem fashionably set by a local goldsmith back home.

OUTDOOR CLOTHING

There's an old Nordic saying: there's no such thing as bad weather, just bad clothing. *Akubra* hats (the word means

Didgeridoos and all-weather hats make great souvenirs

"head cover") are designed to cope with all kinds of weather. *Akubra* is a long-standing Australian brand that produces wide-brimmed, felt hats made from the finest rabbit fur. The hats protect the wearer from the scorching sun as well as downpours and sandstorms, and should really be bought at the start of your trip. *Akubras* can be found in all sorts of shapes in hat shops or outdoor outfitters such as R.M. Williams, Ray's Outdoors or Kathmandu. Quality *akubras* – and only these can deal with the extremes of the Australian weather – come at a price. The same is true of *drizabones*, the waxed coats in which stockmen in the outback face the elements; or indeed leather ankle boots that protect your feet over impassable terrain. But just as a warning, those last two might well send the weight of your suitcase skyrocketing!

CROCODILE LEATHER

Belts, bags, wallets or boots: products made from the leather of farmed animals are not a problem to import into Europe providing you have the relevant certificates. The export of kangaroo or possum pelts is also allowed. This is not the case for coral or shells of protected sea creatures, the export of which is prohibited.

SURF'S UP

Feeling the pull of the waves? Pick pretty much any coastline suitable for surfing and you'll find surf shops and schools that not only offer courses, but also rent and sell all the right gear (boards and wetsuits). The most popular manufacturers include Quiksilver, Billabong and Hurley. For reasonably priced boards and clothing, try Anaconda outdoor shops, for example.

SPORT & ACTIVITIES

On the Australian continent, sport is more a way of life than a hobby. And when you can practise sport in the country's huge natural playgrounds, then the possibilities are endless. You can swim, surf, sail and dive in many places around the virtually infinite coastline, and in the mountains you can go climbing and even skiing. The many national parks offer endless hikes, from a short stroll to multi-day tours. Even extreme-sports enthusiasts are sure to get their money's worth.

CANOEING & KAYAKING

Australia's coastline and the rivers of Tasmania or the Snowy Mountains are ideal for sea kayaking, canoeing and rafting. There are many businesses in the hundreds of coastal resorts or on the edge of national parks that have canoes, kayaks and equipment for hire or which organise guided tours. *World Expeditions (worldexpeditions. com.au)* offer tours lasting anything from one day to two weeks *(approx. A\$3300/6 days)* everywhere in Australia, often taking in visits to Aboriginal communities.

DIVING

Apart from the Barrier Reef *(diving queensland.com)*, a household name in itself, there are plenty of other interesting diving areas. Ningaloo Reef in Western Australia is fantastic and far less crowded. Trial courses are a good way to familiarise yourself with this sport. A five-day basic course on the Great Barrier Reef costs around A\$1020 and is offered, for example, by *Pro Dive Cairns (tel. 07 40 31 52 55 | prodivecairns.com)*. Further information is available from *PADI (Professional Association of Diving Instructors | padi.com)*

Riding the waves at Surfer's Paradise

HIKING

The national parks are full of fabulous walking trails, most of them well signposted. Maps are available from the local tourist information centres. Some bushwalks require you to sign out at the local ranger's office before you set off, and leave information on your planned route and expected date of return with them.

Well-known bushwalks include the *Coast Track* through the Royal National Park (two days) near Sydney, the *K'gari (Fraser Island) Great Walk* (six to eight days) in Queensland, and the *Overland Track* (six days) and the *Three Capes Track* (four days) in Tasmania. South Australia offers the *KI Wilderness Trail* (five days) as well as walks through the Flinders Ranges, while the *Cape to Cape Track* (five to seven days) near Margaret River and the *Coastal Trail* in Cape Le Grand National Park (one to two days) are a good choice in Western Australia.

Australia's hiking trails are always extremely well signposted and hard to miss. That said, hikers still get lost in the wilderness from time to time. Given the vast areas and sometimes extreme weather involved, this can end very badly, and those with little hiking experience should book a guided tour *(worldexpeditions.com. au)*. General information: *auswalk. com.au | bushwalkingaustralia.org | greatwalksofaustralia.com.au.*

KITESURFING

With its seemingly endless miles of deserted beaches, Australia is a paradise for kitesurfers, with a choice of spots ranging from sheltered to actively windswept, depending on your experience and appetite for risk. Kiter hotspots include the bays and beaches of Noosaville (Gold Coast), St Kilda and Brighton (Melbourne), Port Douglas (north of Cairns) and

Yallingup (south of Perth). For more information, go to *surfertoday.com*.

MOUNTAIN BIKING

Although the options for conventional cycle tours on the continent are limited – not least because of the distances – there are many areas that offer the ideal terrain for mountain bikers. There is even a 14-km prepared trail on the Whitsunday Island of South Molle. In the Blue Mountains, the hilly 120-km route from Glenbrook to Wentworth is quite a challenge. Twenty routes are outlined by *cycle trailsaustralia.com*, while the macazine *Australian Mountain Bike* contains plenty of interesting information *(ambmag.com.au)*. There are numerous guided tours, while *Outback Cycling (tel. 08 89 52 15 41 | outbackcycling.com)* rents bikes at Uluru, offering tours from Alice Springs to the MacDonnell Ranges; prices start at A\$1150 for four days.

RIDING

You can ride almost anywhere in Australia: in parks, on cattle or sheep stations (hacks often being part of a stay-on-a-farm package), on beaches and through rainforests – or in a rider's paradise, the Snowy Mountains, for example with *Reynella Rides (3 days/4 nights from A\$1150 | tel. 02 64 54 23 86 | reynellarides.com)*.

SAILING

There are sailing schools and associations in all large Australian towns on the coast and in many resorts where you can learn to sail or, for those with more experience, sail as a member of the crew. You can get information and price lists at local visitor information offices.

Sailing in Sydney Harbour is fun even for those who are not fully seaworthy. *Sail Australia (Cremorne | Sydney | tel. 04 18 76 89 06 | sail australia.com.au)* organises sailing charters (from A\$700 for up to seven people). Another fabulous sailing area is the Whitsunday Islands; one renowned organiser of trips from Airlie Beach is *Pro Sail (tel. 07 49 46 75 33 | prosail.com.au)* who offers two days from A\$359.

STAND-UP PADDLEBOARDING

Whether on calm lakes or the waves of the Pacific, stand-up paddling is one

Get up close and personal with a green sea turtle on the Great Barrier Reef

of the most popular watersports in the country. More and more places are offering boards and paddles for hire, so visitors can also try their luck on the water. Those with little experience should start out on calm waters. *Jervis Bay Stand Up Paddle (mob. 04 03 35 47 16 | jervisbaystanduppaddle. com.au)* offers introductory courses followed by a tour (A$75/90 mins).

SURFING

There are surf schools on most of the monitored beaches in Australia. *Let's Go Surfing (tel. 02 93 44 61 00 | safesurfschools.com.au)* on the beach at Maroubra organises excellent introductory courses for A$69 for two hours,

INSIDER TIP
First surf lessons

including surfboard and wetsuit. Surf & stay is offered by *Mojo Surf (tel. 02 66 39 51 00 | mojosurf.com)* on the east coast in Byron Bay: five days including accommodation, full board, equipment and lessons for A$775.

Surfies meet up on the beaches of the Great Ocean Road, preferably Bells Beach, the Gold Coast or at the southern end of the west coast, where the waves are notoriously strong and therefore only for experienced surfers.

By contrast, the waters around Perth are perfect for beginners, while Moana beach in southern Adelaide is also an ideal place to learn to surf, for example with *Surf & Sun (surfandsun. com.au)*. Find out more about the top spots at *surfing-waves.com* and *surfing australia.com*.

REGIONAL OVERVIEW

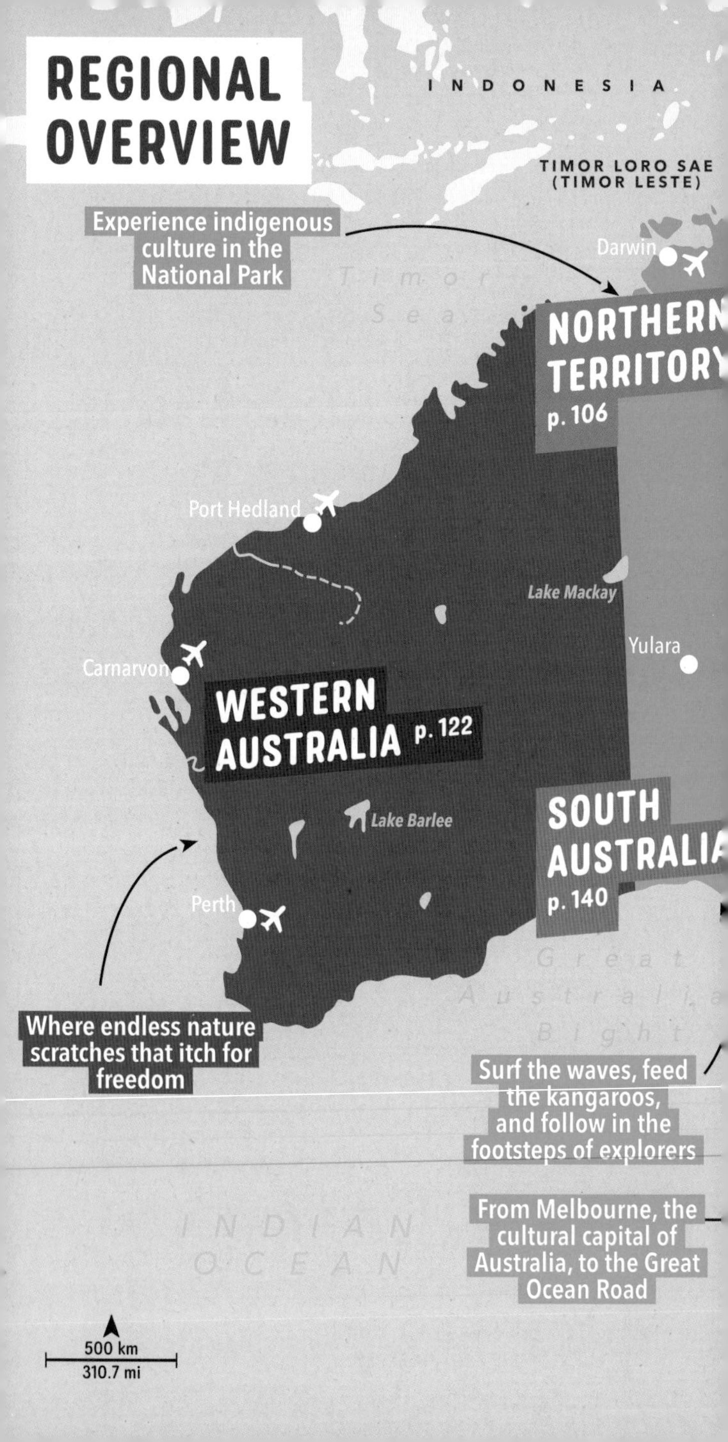

INDONESIA

TIMOR LORO SAE
(TIMOR LESTE)

Experience indigenous culture in the National Park

Darwin

Timor Sea

NORTHERN TERRITORY
p. 106

Port Hedland

Lake Mackay

Yulara

Carnarvon

WESTERN AUSTRALIA p. 122

Lake Barlee

SOUTH AUSTRALIA
p. 140

Perth

Great Australian Bight

Where endless nature scratches that itch for freedom

Surf the waves, feed the kangaroos, and follow in the footsteps of explorers

From Melbourne, the cultural capital of Australia, to the Great Ocean Road

INDIAN OCEAN

500 km
310.7 mi

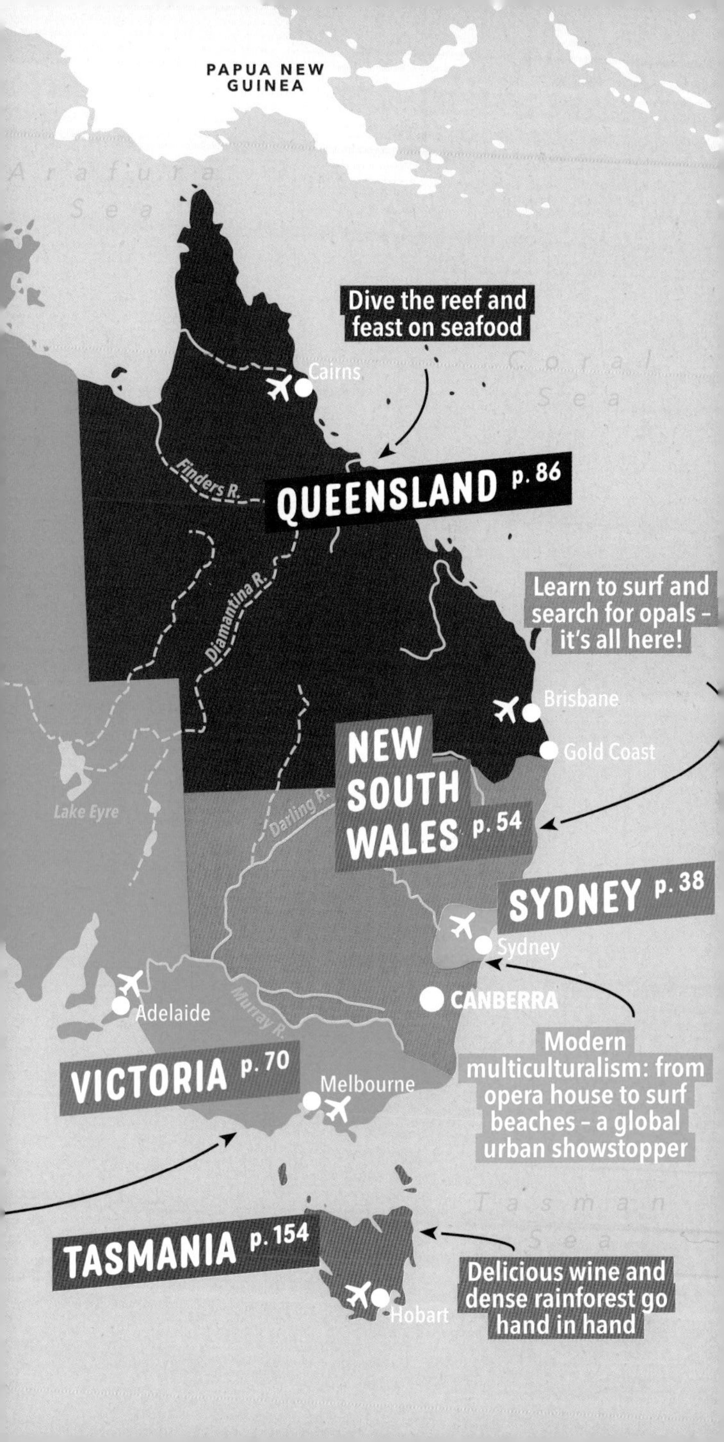

PAPUA NEW GUINEA

Arafura Sea

Coral Sea

Dive the reef and feast on seafood

Cairns

Flinders R.

QUEENSLAND p. 86

Diamantina R.

Learn to surf and search for opals – it's all here!

Brisbane

Gold Coast

Lake Eyre

Darling R.

NEW SOUTH WALES p. 54

SYDNEY p. 38

Sydney

Adelaide

Murray R.

CANBERRA

Modern multiculturalism: from opera house to surf beaches – a global urban showstopper

VICTORIA p. 70

Melbourne

Tasman Sea

TASMANIA p. 154

Delicious wine and dense rainforest go hand in hand

Hobart

SYDNEY

BAREFACED BEAUTY

Few cities can offer a welcome to rival that of Sydney. After an interminable flight, you step off the train or airport shuttle at Circular Quay, and there it all is, right in front of your eyes: the buzzing harbour, the striking Opera House and the Harbour Bridge, nicknamed "the coat hanger" by the locals. Welcome to Sydney!

Australia's busiest metropolis stretches around the natural harbour like an oversized patchwork quilt, covering an area even bigger

Sydney's skyline is impressive by day and breathtaking by night

than that of London. And there's no need to worry about getting bored: you could happily spend months here discovering the countless pretty beach suburbs, exploring museums, browsing the markets, admiring sumptuous mansion houses or sampling your way through the city's many gastronomic delights.

But who has that much time? Focus on what you know you want to see, and make sure you take time to simply soak up the atmosphere of this cosmopolitan showstopper of a city.

SYDNEY

Blue Mountains National Park ★

5 Harbour Bridge ★

2 Opera House ★

Opera Kitchen

The Rocks ★
6

Phillip's Foote

1 Circular Quay ★

Justice & Police Museum **4**

3 Royal Botanic Gardens ★

Bridge Room

Kasino The Star

Art Gallery of
New South Wales **7**

Manta

Sea Life
Sydney Aquarium **12**

King Street

Harry's Café de Wheels

Sydney Tower Eye **10**

8 Hyde Park Barracks

Bambini Trust

13 Kings Cross

11 Darling Harbour ★

9 Australian Museum

Pier Street

Oxford Street

George Street

Darlinghurst Road

Head Road

Wattle Street

Albion Street

22

Foveaux Street

36

Moore Park Road

Oxford Street

Cleveland Street

Street

Il Baretto

Cleveland Street

Regent Street

Redfern Street

Baptist Street

South Dowling Street

Driver Avenue

Anzac Parade

Mitchell Road

Wyndham Street

Elizabeth

Dacey Avenue

Taronga Zoo

Manly Beach

MARCO POLO HIGHLIGHTS

★ **CIRCULAR QUAY**
Just round the corner from the Opera House, this is the beating heart of the city ➤ p. 42

★ **OPERA HOUSE**
The crown jewel in the urban showstopper that is Sydney ➤ p. 43

★ **ROYAL BOTANIC GARDENS**
Caution: loud noises! Especially when the bats wake up at dusk ➤ p. 43

★ **HARBOUR BRIDGE**
Steel steps and ladders let you explore this Sydney landmark ➤ p. 44

★ **THE ROCKS**
Historic pubs, lively restaurants and great shops ➤ p. 44

★ **DARLING HARBOUR**
Spend an evening in Sydney's liveliest harbour ➤ p. 46

★ **BLUE MOUNTAINS NATIONAL PARK**
The wilderness on Sydney's doorstep ➤ p. 52

Bradleys Head Road

ince Albert Street

Old South Head Road

Towns Road

Old South Head Road

Hardy Street

Street

Street

Syd Einfeld Drive

Ebley Street

Birrell Street

Road

Darley Road

Carrington Road

Murray Street

Bondi Road

Old South Head Road

Blair Street

Bondi Beach

Bronte Beach

Tasman Sea

800 m
875 yd

Jacaranda blossom and palm trees in the Royal Botanic Gardens

Culture, skyscrapers and beaches: for many people, both locals and visitors, Sydney is the most beautiful harbour city in the world. The white "shell" roof of the Opera House glistens in the bright sun, set off against the palm trees in the Botanic Gardens.

Sailing boats and ferries cut across the blue waters of the harbour spanned by the steel arch of the Harbour Bridge. Welcome to the heart of the city with a population of 5 million – it's a vibrant, multicultural metropolis and the capital of the oldest Australian state of New South Wales.

Sydney covers a vast area, stretching more than 100km down the coast and some 70km inland. The local transport system is well developed and the most important sights can be reached on the Explorer Big Bus Sydney *(theaustralienexplorer.com.au)*.

WHERE TO START?

The best starting point is **Circular Quay** at **Sydney Cove**, where the station and bus terminal are, and where the city ferries sail from. You're at the very heart of things here, with the Opera House in front of you and Harbour Bridge behind you. All the ferries and City Rail trains stop here. Driving in the city centre is not recommended.

SIGHTSEEING

1 CIRCULAR QUAY ★

Circular Quay is the main tourist artery of this thriving metropolis. Every day millions of people set off from here to every single corner of Sydney. It's best to travel here by a ferry because the views of the Opera House and Harbour Bridge from the water are sensational. If you want something a little more active, then enjoy *Sydney Harbour* from a kayak. Try a guided kayak tour in a small group with *Sydney Harbour Kayaks (A$89 | sydney harbourkayaks.com.au).* Harbour trips are *offered by Captain Cook Cruises (daily 9.30am–8pm | from A$45, A$55 with cocktail | captaincook.com.au).*

INSIDER TIP
Paddle across the harbour

2 OPERA HOUSE

The glistening shell-like roof of the Opera House, located right on the harbour, has become Sydney's landmark. The Danish architect Jørn Utzon won an architectural prize with his revolutionary design – and the right to build the Opera House in Sydney. After seven years of battling with Australian bureaucrats who said the project was too expensive, Utzon gave up. His work was only completed after a 14-year building period – and with help from the lottery that provided the necessary funding. Apparently Utzon never got to see the finished building.

The opera theatre, the concert hall and several smaller theatres are all housed in the Opera House. The *Junior Adventure Tour (children A$22, adults A$32)* gives younger visitors the chance to let their inner diva or conductor run free. *Other guided tours take place daily 9am–5pm | A$40 | Bennelong Point | sydney*

operahouse.com | bus/City Rail/ferry Circular Quay, on foot along Circular Quay East | ⊙ 1–3 hrs

3 ROYAL BOTANIC GARDENS ⭐

The botanical gardens in Sydney are on the harbour's most beautiful bay, not far from the Opera House. This was where the fields of the first farm in the penal colony were once established. The original section of the gardens with Australian trees and plants was laid out in 1816.

A well-maintained path leads from the Opera House along the waterside to *Lady Macquarie's Chair*, a seat hewn out of the rock which offers an impressive view of the Opera House and Harbour Bridge. Governor Macquarie's wife suffered badly from homesickness and used to sit here watching the ships arriving from her home country. The cool grove of palm trees with countless flying foxes, the herb garden and the Tropical Centre are all fascinating. *Daily 7am until sunset | rbgsyd.nsw.gov.au | City Rail Circular Quay, Martin Place or St James | ⊙ 1 hr*

4 JUSTICE & POLICE MUSEUM

Are you in the mood for a little spookiness? Then pay a visit to the museum of Sydney's gangsters and crooks in the former home of the water police. The restored magistrates court, several remand cells and a collection of murder weapons, as well as artefacts belonging to the legendary Ned Kelly Gang are among the highlights. *Sat, Sun 10am–5pm | A$12 | Albert Street/ Phillip Street | short.travel/aus4 | bus/ City Rail/ferry Circular Quay | ⊙ 1 hr*

5 HARBOUR BRIDGE ★

Harbour Bridge is to Sydney what the Statue of Liberty is to New York. For generations of migrants, it was the much-longed-for sign that their journey was finally over: the symbol of freedom and new beginnings. In recent decades, it has above all been a magnet for keen travellers who opt to climb the 1,332 steps of the outer arch of the bridge. The *Bridge Climb (from A$303 | 5 Cumberland Street | The Rocks | tel. 02 82 74 77 77 | bridgeclimb.com)* may be expensive, but it's also an experience that you will never forget. Book ahead!

INSIDER TIP
A small price for a great view

Is your budget tight? For spectacular views of the city, harbour and Opera House, try the Pylon Lookout *(daily 10am–5pm | A$15 | Bridge Stairs | Cumberland Street | The Rocks | pylon lookout.com.au)*. You can reach the Pylon from The Rocks.

6 THE ROCKS ★

The Rocks at the western end of Circular Quay is the oldest part of Sydney. In 1788, convicts erected the city's first proper buildings on solid rock foundations. The sandstone structures that now line the quay and the narrow, cobbled streets date from the early to mid-19th century. In the 1970s the historical buildings were to be demolished to make way for modern skyscrapers. The Builders Labourers' Federation, however, refused to knock them down. In those days the police were sent in; today

The Rocks is a conservation area. In the meantime, tourists have made the quarter their own. No wonder, with the wonderful location close to Circular Quay and all its pubs and restaurants.

Visit the *Rocks Discovery Museum (daily 10am–5pm | admission free | 2–8 Kendall Lane | ☉ 0.5 hr)*, where Australia's history goes back to before the European invasion, and at the weekend head to the *Market on George Street*. If you'd like to know more, a free 90-minute tour of The Rocks departs

INSIDER TIP
Free tour

daily at 6pm from *Cadman's Cottage (110 George Street)*. Spot the tour guides by their green T-shirt. *therocks. com | Bus/City Rail/ferry Circular Quay*

7 ART GALLERY OF NEW SOUTH WALES 🐾

Amazing: In 1874 – only a few decades after the transportation of the first convicts, and with a population of only 200,000 – a respectable art gallery opens in the middle of Sydney that is still one of the biggest in Australia today. Be sure to visit *Yiribana*, the largest exhibition of Aboriginal Australian art in the world. *Daily 10am–5pm | admission free, free guided tours on enquiry | Art Gallery Road | The Domain | artgallery.nsw.gov.au | Sydney Explorer Bus stop 7 | ⏱ 1 hr*

INSIDER TIP
Indigenous artists

8 HYDE PARK BARRACKS

If walls could speak, then these ancient ones, built by convicts, would have plenty to say – probably not much that is cheerful, though. At least 50,000 convicts are said to have passed through the dismal gates, checked over and ordered to work. After transportation of convicts ended in the second half of the 19th century, the building was used as an orphanage for Irish girls who had escaped the great famine. Their poignant stories live on in the moving museum. *Daily 10am–5pm | A$12 | Queens Square/Macquarie Street | short.travel/aus13 | Sydney Explorer Bus stop 11 | ⏱ 1 hr*

The view of the Harbour Bridge and the Opera House is particularly beautiful at sunset

Watch sharks and turtles from below the waterline at the Sea Life Sydney Aquarium

9 AUSTRALIAN MUSEUM

Carnivorous giant kangaroos, monster wombats and dinosaurs with razor-sharp teeth – Sydney's natural history museum provides a fascinating and often humorous look at the evolutionary history of the Australian continent and its people and animals. *Daily 9.30am–5pm | A$15 | 1 William Street | australianmuseum.net.au | Sydney Explorer Bus stop 3 | ⏱ 1 hr*

10 SYDNEY TOWER EYE

Did you know? Covering an area of more than 12,000km², Sydney is almost eight times the size of London. Very difficult to imagine – unless you happen to be standing 250m up, on the lookout platform of the Sydney Tower Eye, and gazing over the almost endless ocean of skyscrapers, detached homes and well-tended parks. That's all very nice, but where's the kick? That awaits on the *Skywalk*, a 45-minute tour around the tower, in the open air and partly on glass walkways. *Daily 9am–10pm | admission A$29, A$70 including Skywalk, cheaper online | access from the Centrepoint Shopping Centre, Level 5 | 100 Market Street | City Rail/bus St James | ⏱ 1 hr*

11 DARLING HARBOUR ★

According to legend, the harbour shore was once known as The Hungry Mile, a reference to the waterside workers searching for work along the wharves each day. Hunger doesn't tend to be the problem today – unless, of course, you can resist the aromas wafting from the many and varied cuisines. Darling Harbour also offers all kinds of entertainment, including a casino, IMAX cinema, the Aquarium, Wildlife World and Madame Tussauds wax museum. If you're travelling with children, make sure to reserve extra time for the 👥 water playground at the southern end of the harbour – the kids will never forgive you if you miss it! *darlingharbour.com | ferry from Circular Quay | Sydney Explorer Bus stops 15, 16 and 17*

12 SEA LIFE SYDNEY AQUARIUM 📍👥

The transparent tunnel takes you through an undersea world. The artificial Barrier Reef with its tropical fish and classical music is simply stunning. *Daily 9.30am–6pm | from A$44, online from A$35 | Aquarium Pier | Darling Harbour | sydneyaquarium. com.au | ferry Aquarium Pier | Sydney Explorer Bus stop 19 | ⏱ 1.5 hrs*

13 KINGS CROSS

Urban development has long since given this old Sydney neighbourhood an innocent look, but the legends of its rough past as a red-light district live on. Today "The Cross" is above all an entertainment centre for Sydneysiders who like to spend their evenings in popular pubs and nightclubs. However, it also offers backpackers' accommodation and inexpensive restaurants. *City Rail T4 Kings Cross*

14 TARONGA ZOO

Let's be honest: do giraffes really need this fabulous view? Maybe not, but it certainly makes for fabulous photographs: long giraffe necks at the front of the picture, the Opera House in the background. And when you do manage to drag your eyes away from the view, be sure to visit the flying display and the sea lions. *Daily 9.30am–5pm | A$46, online A$42 | Head Road | Bradleys | taronga.org.au | ferry from Circular Quay (free in combination with a zoo ticket) | ⏱ 2 hrs*

EATING & DRINKING

Where there are tourists, there is food: and you certainly won't be hungry for long at Darling Harbour or on Circular Quay, where you'll find one restaurant after another. You can fill up for slightly less in Kings Cross or in the suburbs Glebe, Newtown or Surry Hills. If you fancy seafood, don't miss a visit to *Sydney Fish Market (10am–5pm every day | Pyrmont Bridge Road/Bank Street | City Rail Fish Market)* for a delicious waterfront lunch of fresh prawns and oysters.

INSIDER TIP Fresh out of the water

BAMBINI TRUST

Exquisite food and atmosphere, with coffee specially flown in from Italy; the steaks and fresh seafood are a favourite with regulars. Tip: order a *coffee/latte to go* and head for Albert Park close by. *Mon–Fri from 7am, Sat from 5.30pm | 185 Elizabeth Street | tel. 02 92 83 70 98 | bambinitrust.com.au | $$$ | City Rail Martin Place*

IL BARETTO

Not expensive and yet very good – Sydneysiders love such places, which means it is always packed at any time of day. Serves specialities from northern Italy as well as pasta dishes and pizzas. *Closed Sun |496 Bourke Street | tel. 02 93 61 61 63 | $–$$ | bus 389 Darlinghurst (Stanley Street)*

BRIDGE ROOM

Not a fine dining atmosphere, but stylish and authentic. The specialities are unusual fish and seafood dishes such as *Fraser Island spanner crab* (a crab from the Australian coastal waters). *Closed Mon, evenings only on Sat | 44 Bridge Street | tel. 02 92 47 70 00 | thebridgeroom.com. au | $$$ | bus 555 Loftus Street*

HARRY'S CAFÉ DE WHEELS

Not exactly a location for gourmets, but oh-so Aussie: Harry's has been serving its famous pies for decades – with all sorts of Australian meat fillings as well as other variations. *Daily from 8.30am | Tumbalong Park | tel. 02 92 11 72 94 | $ | City Rail Town Hall*

MANTA

The decor is unpretentious – black wooden tables, white walls and few pictures. The same goes for the food: fresh oysters are served without any frills as is the Arab-style octopus. *Daily | The Wharf at Woolloomooloo | Cowper Wharf Road | tel. 02 93 32 38 22 | $$$ | bus 311 Potts Point*

OPERA KITCHEN

We know what you're thinking: a tourist trap. But the burgers and Asian dishes are surprisingly fresh, and yes – the location right under the Opera House with views of Harbour Bridge is unbeatable. The adjoining open-air bar is very popular for a sundowner. *Daily from 7.30am | Lower Concourse Level | Bennelong Point | operakitchen. com.au | $–$$ | bus/City Rail/ferry Circular Quay*

SHOPPING

For the more stylish shoppers, the *Strand Arcade (255 Pitt Street | City Rail Town Hall)* and the ⚑ *Queen Victoria Building (455 George Street | City Rail Town Hall)* house expensive boutiques, designer shops and tea rooms.

Unconventional fashions can be found on *King Street (bus 422 Newtown)* in Newtown and *Glebe Point Road (bus 433 near Hereford Street)* in the student district of Glebe. Several top Australian designers have boutiques on *Oxford Street (bus 333 Darlinghurst Road)* in Paddington. This is also where the most popular *market* in the city is held every Saturday around St John's Church *(paddingtonmarkets.com.au).* This is a great spot to pick up some nifty souvenirs from local artisans. Aboriginal art, everything from murals to boomerangs, is available from *Karlangu Aboriginal Art Centre (47 York Street | karlangu.com | City Rail Wynyard).*

Find accessories to match your travel outfits at the market in Paddington

SPORT & ACTIVITIES

You can easily leave the city behind you, even on foot, for example on the *Federation Cliff Walk*, a 5-km path along the coast, from the eastern residential area of Dover Heights, past the sandstone cliffs to Watson Bay. If you're still feeling energetic, you can take the 6-km *Coastal Walk* from Bondi to Coogee, or enjoy the views of *North Head Walk* in Manly. *short. travel/aus34*.

Sydney is famous for its beautiful pools built into the sea, the oldest of which is more than 200 years old. Take a dip at 🐖 *Bronte Baths* or 🐖 *Cronulla Rock Pool* – both free of charge. The *Cook+Phillip Park Pool* in the city has a great fitness and wellness programme *(Mon–Fri, 6am–10pm, Sat & Sun, 7am–8pm | pool entry A$7.70, fitness session approx. A$20 | William Street | cookandphillip.org.au | City Rail St James)*.

BEACHES

Sydney's more than 30 beaches stretch almost 100km down the coast. 🦅 *Bondi Beach*, the most famous and now on the National Heritage List, can be reached by bus, as can the other beaches *(transportnsw.info)*. There is less going on at *Tamarama*, 🦅 *Bronte* and *Clovelly Beach*. *Coogee Beach* is a pretty, family-friendly beach with hotels, restaurants and cafés. Some beaches also have rock pools, perfect for relaxing in, such as *Maroubra*, where you can treat yourself to a cup of coffee afterwards in *Pavilion Beachfront (daily | Fitzgerald Av. | pavilionbeachfront.com.au)*. The waves at

Start your night at the Lord Nelson

BARS & PUBS

The most typical watering holes are in *The Rocks*. *The Australian (100 Cumberland Street)* and *The Lord Nelson (19 Kent Street)* and *The Argyle (12 Argyle Street)* have remained unspoilt, the first two also serving their own delicious home-brewed beer. *Establishment Bar (248–252 George Street | bus/City Rail/ferry Circular Quay)* on the ground floor of the eponymous boutique hotel is one of the hotspots of the "in" scene. There's often live music in the city's oldest pub, the *Fortune of War (137 George Street | ferry/City Rail Circular Quay)* on Thursday to Sunday evenings.

Manly Beach are up to 1.6m high. If you're not a strong swimmer, then take a few steps south to *Shelly Beach*, which is sheltered.

BALMORAL BEACH

This is the place to come if you want to avoid exposing your little ones to the rough east coast surf. The bay of this pretty suburb is sheltered to the harbour's north. While the kids build sandcastles, parents can soak in the view over lunch or a coffee at *Bathers' Pavilion (daily | tel. 02 99 69 50 50 | batherspavilion.com.au | $$$).*

NIGHTCLUBS

Nightlife centres on *Oxford Street* and the neighbouring districts of *Paddington* and *Kings Cross*. Clubs that are often open until around 5am, especially at weekends, include *Kinselas (383 Bourke Street | bus 389 near Burton Street)*; *Candys Apartment (22 Bayswater Road | City Rail Kings Cross)*, *Oxford Hotel (134 Oxford Street | bus 333 Oxford Street, corner of Darlinghurst Road)*.

THE STAR

Casinos are hugely popular in Australia. Experience the magic for yourself as you stand in front of the glittering entrance to the Star Casino and its shopping arcade. *80 Pyrmont Street | star.com.au | Explorer Bus stop 15*

OPEN-AIR CINEMA

Australians love open-air cinemas. In Sydney these are *St George Open Air Cinema (Mrs Macquarie's Chair | Jan/Feb | A$38 | stgeorgeopenair.com.au)* in the Royal Botanic Garden; *Moonlight Cinema (in Centennial Park | Dec–Mar | A$19 | moonlight.com.au | City Rail Bondi Junction)*; and *Bondi Openair Cinema (Jan–March | from A$35 | openaircinemas.com.au)* on the beach promenade with music played beforehand.

THEATRE

Company B/Belvoir Street Theatre (25 Belvoir Street | tel. 02 96 99 34 44 | belvoir.com.au | City Rail Central Station) is a leading theatre company that has produced the likes of Mel Gibson.

Lifeguards are always at the ready on Sydney's beaches

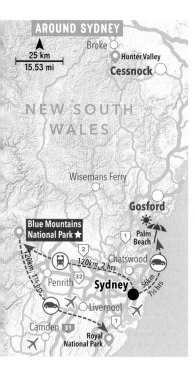

AROUND SYDNEY

25 km
15.53 mi

Broke

Hunter Valley
Cessnock

NEW SOUTH WALES

Wisemans Ferry

Gosford

Blue Mountains National Park ★

Palm Beach

Penrith

120km, 2 hrs

Chatswood

Sydney

56km 1¾ hrs

Liverpool

Camden

Royal National Park

gateway to a city of millions. After Yellowstone in California, "The Royal" was the second national park in the world – a fabulous haven of nature that is just a little smaller than Liechtenstein. Countless walking trails meander through the bush and forests, the cliffs falling steeply down to the ocean. *The Royal National Park Visitor Centre (2 Lady Carrington Drive | Audley | tel. 02 95 42 06 48)* has information on hiking trails and other activities. Travel here by *Cronulla Ferries (cronullaferries.com.au)* to Bundeena. *Daily from 7am–8.30pm | National Park fee A$12 per car and per day | short.travel/aus35 | ▢ J6*

BLUE MOUNTAINS NATIONAL PARK ★
120km / 2 hrs from Sydney by train and bus

The wild Blue Mountains start west of Sydney. The Three Sisters, an impressive rock formation near the little town of Katoomba, are of considerable spiritual importance to the local Aboriginal people. Wonderful views over deep gorges and the forested mountain ranges in the national park can be had from Echo Point, not far from the spectacular Three Sisters.

Just 1km or so away on the western outskirts of Katoomba, *Scenic World (daily 9am–5pm | A$39, Sat, Sun A$43 for the all-inclusive Unlimited Discovery Pass | scenicworld.com.au)* combines breathtaking views with a bit of excitement. The more daring can take the *Scenic Railway* that plunges 415m down a steep incline, then the *Scenic Skyway*, a cablecar across the

Roslyn Packer Theatre Walsh Bay (22 Hickson Road/Millers Point | The Rocks | tel. 02 92 50 19 99 | roslyn packertheatre.com.au | bus/City Rail/ ferry Circular Quay)

At the *Opera House (see p. 43)* you can see opera, comedy, dance and theatre *(box office 02 92 50 71 11)*.

AROUND SYDNEY

ROYAL NATIONAL PARK
36km / 50 mins from Sydney by car
It's hard to believe you're at the

gorge far below, the *Scenic Cableway*, another panoramic cablecar ride up or down and hike along the well-maintained 3-km *Scenic Walkway* through the rainforest.

Information and maps are available from the *NPWS Blue Mountains Heritage Centre (Govetts Leap Road | Blackheath | tel. 02 47 87 88 77 | visit bluemountains.com.au)*. Various bus companies run day trips from Sydney. If you arrive by train from *Central Station (sydneytrains.info)*, you can take the *Explorer Bus (explorerbus. com.au)* that starts at Katoomba and stops at the major sights. ▢ *H6*

PALM BEACH
56km / 1hr 15 mins from Sydney by car

Time to escape the city. A good hour's drive north of the city centre is the suburb of Palm Beach on a headland stretching out into the sea. Particularly beautiful and usually far less crowded than beaches closer to the city is the ✿ *beach* directly south of Barrenjoey Lighthouse. While you're in this neck of the woods, stop for a short *walk* in the idyllic *Ku-ring-gai Chase National Park*, where you'll find (rain)forest and heathland galore. ▢ *J6*

HUNTER VALLEY
120km / 2 hrs from Sydney by car

The Hunter Valley is the oldest wine-growing region in Australia with more than 50 award-winning wineries *(winecountry.com.au)*, producing delicate, fruity white wines and some reds (Pinot Noir and Shiraz). Many wineries also have first-class restaurants – and luxurious accommodation. ▢ *H–J6*

A GOOD NIGHT'S SLEEP

LIKE STAYING WITH OLD FRIENDS

Are you hoping to stay for longer than just a day trip in the Blue Mountains? Your best bet is *Lurline House (7 rooms | 122 Lurline Street | tel. 02 47 82 46 09 | lurlinehouse. com.au | $$)* in the heart of Katoomba. Built in 1910, Lurline House has retained its neat and tidy charm from the old days. You'll sleep in a cosy four-poster bed in the small, friendly family-run guesthouse and be treated to a delicious breakfast when you wake, plus the best conditions for a hike to Echo Point.

ROUGHING IT IN LUXURY WITH A HARBOUR VIEW

Admittedly, this isn't really budget travel, but what is more popular in Sydney than the impressive view of the Opera House and harbour? At *Sydney Harbour YHA (106 rooms | 110 Cumberland Street | tel. 02 82 72 09 00 | yha.com.au | $$ | bus/ City Rail/ferry Circular Quay)*, you can enjoy it from one of the sun loungers on the roof terrace of this luxury hostel with its comfortable dorms and double rooms with bathrooms, large clean kitchen and inviting common rooms. Book well in advance!

NEW SOUTH WALES

A LITTLE BIT OF EVERYTHING

Endless beaches, eucalyptus forests around romantic lakes, isolated farms and cattle stations, subtropical heat in huge national parks that encompass landscapes ranging from desert to rainforest, and freezing temperatures in the Snowy Mountains – all this is New South Wales.

The "First State", at 801,600 km² and more than three times the size of the UK, is the oldest and most densely populated state in Australia – although outside Sydney, with its population of

Experience the intense greenery of the rainforest in Dorrigo National Park

five million, you don't really notice this. There are lots of empty beaches along its 1,000-km-long coastline; you can hike for days in the Snowy Mountains without ever meeting a soul, and in the pubs in the outback, strangers are still something of a novelty. For many visitors who land at Sydney airport, the fascinating state capital overshadows the "rest" of New South Wales. But the state has a lot more going for it.

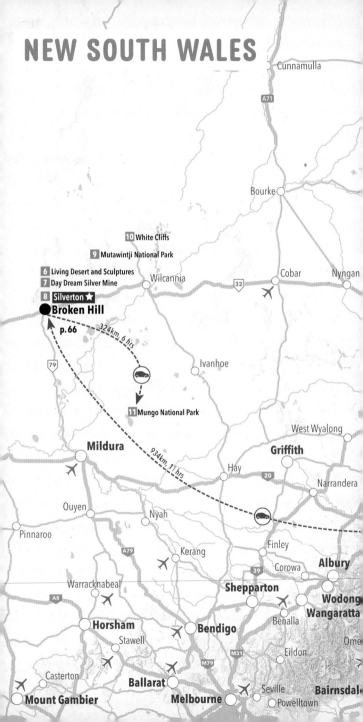

NEW SOUTH WALES

Cunnamulla

A71

Bourke

10 White Cliffs

9 Mutawintji National Park

6 Living Desert and Sculptures
7 Day Dream Silver Mine

8 Silverton ★

● **Broken Hill**

Wilcannia

Cobar

Nyngan

32

p. 66

79

324km, 6 hrs

Ivanhoe

11 Mungo National Park

934km, 11 hrs

West Wyalong

Mildura

Griffith

Hay

20

Narrandera

Ouyen

Nyah

Pinnaroo

A79

Kerang

Finley

Corowa

Albury

Warracknabeal

Shepparton

39

Benalla

Wodong
Wangaratta

A8

Horsham

Stawell

Bendigo

M79

Eildon

Ome

Casterton

Ballarat

M31

Seville

Bairnsdal

Mount Gambier

Melbourne

Powelltown

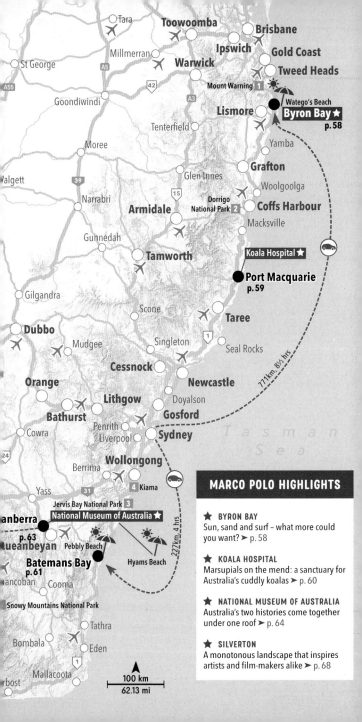

Tara
Toowoomba
Brisbane
Ipswich
Gold Coast
Millmerran
Warwick
Tweed Heads
St George
Mount Warning
Watego's Beach
Goondiwindi
Byron Bay ★
p.58
Tenterfield
Lismore
Yamba
Moree
Grafton
Glen Innes
Woolgoolga
Narrabri
Dorrigo
National Park
Coffs Harbour
Armidale
Macksville
Gunnedah
Koala Hospital ★
Tamworth
Port Macquarie
p.59
Gilgandra
Scone
Taree
Dubbo
Mudgee
Singleton
Seal Rocks
Cessnock
771km, 8½ hrs
Orange
Newcastle
Lithgow
Doyalson
Bathurst
Gosford
Cowra
Penrith
Liverpool
Sydney
Tasman
Sea
Wollongong
Berrima
Kiama
Yass
Jervis Bay National Park
National Museum of Australia ★
Canberra
p.63
Queanbeyan
Pebbly Beach
Batemans Bay
p.61
Hyams Beach
227km, 4 hrs
ancoban
Cooma
Snowy Mountains National Park
Tathra
Bombala
Eden
rbost
Mallacoota

100 km
62.13 mi

MARCO POLO HIGHLIGHTS

★ **BYRON BAY**
Sun, sand and surf – what more could you want? ➤ p. 58

★ **KOALA HOSPITAL**
Marsupials on the mend: a sanctuary for Australia's cuddly koalas ➤ p. 60

★ **NATIONAL MUSEUM OF AUSTRALIA**
Australia's two histories come together under one roof ➤ p. 64

★ **SILVERTON**
A monotonous landscape that inspires artists and film-makers alike ➤ p. 68

BYRON BAY

(◫ J5) **A city with no traffic lights? All the more reason to stop in ★ Byron Bay (pop. 9,500)! With all** motorways. *Main Beach* stretches 50km, almost as far as the Gold Coast in Queensland, whereas ✈ *Watego's Beach* is a dream come true for surfers who ride the breakers alongside dolphins.

Surfers at Byron Bay don't have to wait long for the perfect wave

sorts of water sports, a beautiful hinterland with high mountains and rainforest, as well as a lively pub scene, Byron Bay is a booming tourist destination.

This was once the preserve of backpackers and dropouts – but they have long since moved further inland to Nimbin. It is largely younger, wellheeled tourists who really get things going in the evenings on Bay Street, while during the day surfers enjoy stunning beaches the width of

SIGHTSEEING

CAPE BYRON

This peninsula, named by James Cook on his first trip (1768–71), juts out a long way into the sea. You can drive to the old lighthouse or take the well-maintained path to *Captain Cook Lookout* (3.5km, the entire round trip will take about two hours). From here you have an overwhelming view of Watego's Bay. June and July, and September to November are the best months for whale watching; dolphins play in the water all year round.

EATING & DRINKING

FINS

Fish and fun is the motto, and the reason why Byron Bay trendsetters are happy to drive the 60km to Kingscliff. *Daily in the evenings, Fri–Sun also at lunchtime | 5/6 Bells Blvd | Salt Village | South Kingscliff | tel. 02 66 74 48 33 | fins.com.au | $$$*

MISS MARGARITA

There's never a slow night at this Mexican eatery. Try the *jalapeño poppers*, best with a passionfruit *mojito*. *Daily | 2 Jonson Street | tel. 02 66 85 68 26 | missmargarita.com.au | $$*

AROUND BYRON BAY

The area inland from Byron Bay, with banana plantations, dense rainforest and small villages with a colourful mixture of unconventional shops, is fascinating. From Byron Bay, head first of all for *Mullumbimby*, then take the highway to *Murwillumbah (approx. 50km)*. From here, the roads to *Uki*, *Nimbin*, *Lismore* and the little artists' colony *Bangalow* are narrow and twisty.

🏝 MOUNT WARNING
70km / 1 hr from Byron Bay by car
The turning to *Mount Warning National Park* is between Murwillumbah and Uki. *Mount Warning (mtwarning.net)* is the remnant of a huge volcano that erupted millions of years ago. A unique ecological niche was created between the lava masses where wonderful rainforest and rare flora and fauna now thrive. It is well worth climbing Mount Warning early in the morning when the sun starts to rise above Australia's easternmost point and the surrounding area is bathed in a fascinating light. The tour takes about two hours. Note: the final section should only be tackled if you have a head for heights. Sturdy shoes essential. ▢ *J5*

INSIDER TIP
Up the volcano

PORT MACQUARIE

(▢ *J6*) **Considering the heavenly beaches, it is almost impossible to imagine that this idyllic beachside town was once a penal settlement for convicts who were repeat offenders.**

"Port" (pop. 45,000) is one of the oldest settlements in Australia; a manageable small town that nestles against the Hasting River, and offers a wide range of water sports, mile-long beaches for swimming or surfing, stretching from *Town Beach* and *Oxley Beach* near the town centre to *Lighthouse Beach* in the south.

SIGHTSEEING

KOALA HOSPITAL ★ 👥 🐂

The largest animal clinic of its kind in Australia is run on an honorary basis and often has more than 30 patients. Many of the marsupials taken in here are victims of a road accident or bush fire. After being treated by expert vets and when they have fully recovered, they are released back into the wild. If you're still looking for that special souvenir, how about adopting a koala? Sadly, you don't actually get to take the bear home, but you do get a certificate complete with a picture of your koala (who will be released back into the wild after treatment), with your donation going to the Koala Hospital. They are fed at 3pm. *Daily 8am–4.30pm | admission free, donations gratefully received | Lord Street | koalahospital.org.au |* ⊙ *1 hr*

INSIDER TIP
Adopt a koala!

SEA ACRES RAINFOREST CENTRE

Discover the rainforest. The 1.3-km boardwalk – supposedly the longest wooden walk in the world – is up to 7m above the ground, and it takes you through an unspoilt tropical rainforest at eye level with a whole range of tree-dwellers. *Daily 9am–4.30pm | A$9 | Sea Acres Nature Reserve | short. travel/aus7 |* ⊙ *1.5 hrs*

HASTINGS RIVER

A solid proportion of the oysters sold in Australia are farmed in the waters of Port Macquarie. Some cruises stop at the oyster farms, and dolphins frolic in the water all year round. If you're there between June and September, make sure your camera's to hand for any whale sightings. Join *Port Jet Cruise Adventures (1 Short Street | Town Wharf | tel. 65 83 88 11 | portjet. com.au)* onboard *(from A$20)* or dare to try your luck on a jet ski *(A$110/30 mins rental)*!

EATING & DRINKING

PORT FRESH SEAFOODS

This is where you can find cheap fresh oysters, and other delicacies. *Mon–Fri 9am–5.30pm, Sat until 3pm | 5/23–41 Short Street | tel. 02 65 83 83 48 | portfreshseafoods.com.au*

AROUND PORT MACQUARIE

② DORRIGO NATIONAL PARK

175km / 2 hrs from Port Macquarie by car

The park is 900m up in the mountains of the Great Dividing Range, 180km north of Port Macquarie. It is one of the most beautiful and accessible national parks in New South Wales. The 70m-high skywalk, a 250-m-long path through the tree canopy of the rainforest can be especially recommended. Pick up a fold-out map with all the trails marked at the *Dorrigo Rainforest Centre (daily 9am–5pm | Dome Road | short.travel/aus37)*. A number of artists, craftspeople and

Cute animal portraits are guaranteed at the Koala Hospital

organic farmers have settled in and around the pretty historical village of *Bellingen* (pop. 3,000). Good craft shops and a nice café can be found in the *Old Butter Factory (1 Doepel Street | theoldbutterfactory.com.au).* *J5*

BATEMANS BAY

(*H7*) **Even travellers need a break at some time or another! And where would be better to stop and relax than idyllic Batemans Bay (pop. 16,000) on the south coast?**

This idyllic sunbathing spot is a good starting point for exploring the hidden beaches, fishing villages and national parks along the south coast.

SIGHTSEEING

MURRAMURANG NATIONAL PARK

Now this is what you call down under: a tent under the eucalyptus trees, endless, empty beaches and adorable pygmy kangaroos, far more curious than shy, who will happily jump over to meet you; and all just a 20-minute drive from the seaside town of Batemans Bay. The national park runs down a spectacular stretch of coast with small sandy beaches, steep cliffs and numerous caves. Hikers and fossil hunters in particular will definitely find what they are looking for here. At *Pebbly Beach*, a small, sheltered beach inside the national park, your chances of meeting a pygmy kangaroo are high!

EATING & DRINKING

STARFISH DELI

Incredible food with an even better view at this fish and pizza restaurant right on the water. *Daily | Clyde Street | tel. 02 44 72 48 80 | $$-$$$*

AROUND BATEMANS BAY

3 JERVIS BAY NATIONAL PARK

115km / 1.5 hrs from Batemans Bay by car

North of Batemans Bay is this paradisiacal bay with bright white beaches, crystal-clear water, eucalyptus forests and pockets of rainforest. Kangaroos, wallabies and flying foxes can be seen almost everywhere. Parrots land on the arms and shoulders of anyone who has bird food with them. Dolphins and penguins live in the sheltered bays. If that weren't all enough, whale-watching is possible from May to November: *Dolphin Watch Cruises (from A$35, A$65 in whale season | 50 Owen Street | Huskisson | tel. 02 44 41 63 11 | dolphinwatch.com.au).* Just so you know, Jervis Bay boasts the whitest sandy beach – not just in Australia, but allegedly in the world, with ✺ Hyams Beach even making it into the book of Guinness World Records. *H6-7*

INSIDER TIP
Snow-white sand

4 KIAMA

160km / 4 hrs from Batemans Bay by car

The pretty historical part of this town (pop. 21,000) north of Batemans Bay, follows the rugged cliffs along the coast to *Blowhole*, Kiama's special attraction. And if the weather is right, it really is quite something: when the wind comes from the south-west, the waves crashing against the cliffs are forced through a deep underwater cavern and shoot 60m up through a hole in the rock. *H6*

5 SNOWY MOUNTAINS NATIONAL PARK

317km / 4 hrs from Batemans Bay by car

Welcome to Australia's answer to the Alps! The mountains rising in the hinterland above the south coast are only ever visited by a few foreign tourists. The Snowies, however, are not just a magnet for winter-sports enthusiasts. In summer, you can experience the solitude of the mountains in this huge national park, the likes of which you won't find in Europe. A large part of the "Australian Alps", that stretch as far as Victoria, is a protected area (in New South Wales at the *Mount Kosciuszko National Park*, in Victoria the *Alpine National Park*). The tourist centres are *Cooma*, *Thredbo* and *Jindabyne*.

An unforgettable experience is a ride through the outlying areas of the national park over a period of several days, organised by *Snowy River Horseback Tours (2 days from A$480 | snowyrivertours.com).* *H7*

Jog through the Australian capital

CANBERRA

(□□ H7) **Canberra (pop. 381,000) is the result of a compromise between Sydney and Melbourne after they could not agree on which city should become the capital.**

It was literally built in the middle of nowhere. "Canberry" – the meeting place – was what the Aboriginal people called the area. The American architects Walter Burley Griffin and Marion Mahony Griffin won the commission to build the city in 1912. Canberra is characterised by its strict geometrical design. The city itself and its suburbs cover about a quarter of the 2,400km² of the total area in the Australian Capital Territory (ACT), which does not belong to the state of New South Wales, but has its own administration. Canberra has two hearts: the northern district around *London Circuit* and the southern one around *Capital Hill*, where parliament stands. A trip to *Mount Ainslie* Lookout provides the best picture of the city. From there you can see the parliamentary district. Interestingly, just a few minutes from the government district is the *Red Hill Nature Reserve*. It's not unusual to spot wild kangaroos out here, where nature is certainly in charge.

SIGHTSEEING

NATIONAL FILM & SOUND ARCHIVE 🐾

The archive is home to key film and audio recordings from the late 19th century onwards. Once you've seen the main exhibition, pop into the small theatre room for fascinating historic short films as well as old cinema and TV classics – all free of charge! *Mon–Thu 9am–5pm, Fri 9am–8pm, Sat & Sun 12–5pm | admission free | McCoy Circuit, Acton Peninsula | nfsa.gov.au | ⏱ 1.5 hrs*

NATIONAL MUSEUM OF AUSTRALIA ★ 🐷

From Aboriginal traditions and Australian fauna to Vegemite – this eye-catching museum is dedicated to Australia's diverse cultures. The interwoven steel "ropes" outside represent the numerous stories that make up Australia. *Daily 9am–5pm | admission free | Lawson Crescent | Acton Peninsula | nma.gov.au | ⏱ 2 hrs*

NATIONAL GALLERY OF AUSTRALIA 🐷

Do not miss this opportunity to see 5,000 years of international art and an excellent collection of Aboriginal Australian works, some up to 30,000 years old. Check out Sidney Nolan's Ned Kelly collection – a central piece of modern Australian art history. *Daily 10am–5pm | admission free | Parkes Place | nga.gov.au | ⏱ 1.5 hrs*

Not a rollercoaster, but one of the "ropes" that feature on the National Museum of Australia

PARLIAMENT HOUSE ⚑

Parliament House is home to the two national parliaments, the House of Representatives, which sits in the green chamber, and the Senate, which has a red colour scheme. The 8m flagpole on the roof has become the symbol of Canberra. Built at a cost of A$1.1 billion, the building – which was opened in 1988 – is the most expensive ever to have been built in Australia. As well as the government, it houses more than 3,000 works of art, many of which are in rooms that are open to the public. 🐷 Free guided tours *(daily 9.30am, 11am, 1pm, 2pm,*

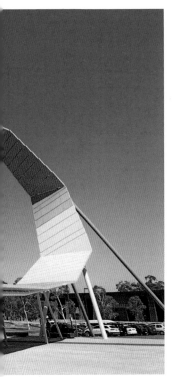

3.30pm | tel. 02 62 77 50 85) can be booked there and then. A visit is particularly interesting at Question Time. Shouting and aggressive remarks between Government and Opposition are not unusual. Information on sessions is available on the website *aph.gov.au.* ⏱ *1.5 hrs*

QUESTACON 👥

This is an absolute must for (budding) scientists or just anyone keen on experiments and testing things out. The science and technology centre offers the chance to experience an earthquake, admire how lightning strikes or trigger a tsunami. *Daily 9am–5pm | A$23, children A$17.50 | King Edward Terrace | questacon.edu. au |* ⏱ *2 hrs*

EATING & DRINKING

AKIBA

Don't put yourself through the misery of trying to choose; instead, ask for the "Just feed me" eight-course meal (vegetarian version also available) with freshly prepared Asian creations. Very popular, so it's a good idea to book in advance! *Daily | 40 Bunda Street | tel. 02 61 62 06 02 | akiba.com.au | $$*

BENTSPOKE

Don't let anyone tell you that nothing ever happens in Canberra. In this hip brewery pub, you'll see an award-winning crankshaft, and dine on excellent salads, burgers and other pub meals. *Daily | 38 Mort Street | Braddon | tel. 02 62 57 52 20 | bent spokebrewing.com.au | $$*

Explore the Living Desert & Sculptures park just outside Broken Hill

NIGHTLIFE

Restaurants and pubs line the modern developed foreshore in the suburb of *Kingston*, so you can enjoy a pleasant stroll from drink to drink along the shore. Braddon has become a hip if slightly small nightlife area.

THE DOCK

Tempura oysters, lychee Martinis, football and live music – the new dock on the banks of Lake Burley Griffin combines the rough Aussie pub atmosphere with class. *Daily | 7 Giles Street | thedockkingston.com.au*

HIPPO CO

Famous for the best Martinis in town. The proprietors also have a soft spot for

good live jazz *(Wed)*. Try the bar's own fruity cocktail creation, the *Is Ryan here?*, or, for something stronger, the *barrel aged Negroni* – both in-house recipes. *Closed Sun | 17 Garema Place*

BROKEN HILL

(▢ G6) **When driving along the highway, Broken Hill (pop. 17,000) suddenly appears out of nowhere: an urban oasis in a desert-like environment.**

This prosperous small town, over 1,100km from Sydney, owes its existence to a farm labourer from Stuttgart in Germany: in 1883, Charles Rasp came across a lode of lead, silver and zinc, which proved to be one of the most lucrative in the world. The slightly collapsed hill – hence the name Broken Hill – became one of the biggest mines, operated by the *Broken Hill Proprietary Company (BHP)*, which became the world's biggest mining company. Despite intensive mining, the reserves are by no means exhausted. *Silver City*, as Broken Hill likes to boast, has a lively art scene and great attractions (including an extremely interesting Flying Doctor base).

Here, by the way, you'll have to adjust your watch. Although the town is in New South Wales, it is in the South Australian time zone.

SIGHTSEEING

LINE OF LODE MINERS MEMORIAL
This memorial to the hundreds of workers who died in the mine is in a fitting location on Federation Hill above the town. Good views, an informative visitor centre and a café. *Daily 6am–9pm | admission free | ⏱ 30 mins*

EATING & DRINKING

BELLS
The retro milk bar has survived since the 1950s and unflinchingly continues to serve all sorts of flavours of non-alcoholic milkshakes and soda spiders as well as ice cream and coffee specialities. *Daily 10am–5.30pm | 160 Patton Street | in the south of the town | tel. 08 80 87 53 80*

SHOPPING

ARTS & CRAFTS
There are so many *art galleries* and *craft shops* in Broken Hill that you can spend days visiting studios and exhibitions here. A list of addresses and contacts is available from the visitor centre.

The "Flying Doctor artist" Howard W Steer's bright and colourful paintings are typical *(721 William Street | howardsteerart.com.au)*. *Pro Hart Gallery* exhibits (and sells) works by the local artist Kevin Charles Hart who died in 2006 *(Mon–Sat 9am–5pm | A$5 | 108 Wyman Street | prohart.com. au)*.

AROUND BROKEN HILL

⑥ LIVING DESERT & SCULPTURES
12km / 16 mins from Broken Hill by car
This modern sculpture park is out in the desert, at the top of a hill and far enough from the lights of the town to show off the colours to their best, especially at sunset. It's about a 20-minute walk from the car park; there is a pay office at the entrance *(A$6 per person; please have the right change). Daily 8.30am–8pm | ⏱ 1 hr. 🗺 G6*

INSIDER TIP
Art at dusk

Bizarre juxtapositions are all part of the experience in Silverton

7 DAY DREAM SILVER MINE

31km / 40 mins from Broken Hill by car

A lot of the history here is actually underground. A guided tour (sturdy shoes necessary) through the narrow, low galleries gives you an impression of the hard and dangerous work in the mine at the end of the 19th century when even children were sent underground. *Tours daily 10am and 11.30am | A$32 | turning signposted off the road to Silverton | daydream mine.com.au |* ⏱ *1.5 hrs.* ▥ *G6*

8 SILVERTON ★

24km / 25 mins from Broken Hill by car

A bizarre, near ghost town from the days when silver was mined on a grand scale here. However, there are still people here, and you'll meet them in the little-changed pub of *Silverton Hotel ($$)*, in the small café

and the unconventional artist studios which have been set up in the deserted buildings and are well worth a visit. Your walk through this dusty place should also include the old cemetery with its marble gravestones.

Silverton is a familiar name in the world of film: the outback setting was used for films such as *Mad Max II* and *Priscilla, Queen of the Desert,* among others. At the *Mundi Mundi Plains*, 7km away (signposted), you look out over an amazingly wide horizon. Rumour has it the view here can stretch so far into the distance you can even see the curvature of the earth. In any case, you can't deny it's a pretty impressive panorama! ▥ *G6*

9 MUTAWINTJI NATIONAL PARK

174km / 3 hrs 20 mins from Broken Hill by car

This nature reserve, spanning almost 70,000 ha, is home to a wealth of cave paintings and petroglyphs left behind by local Aboriginal people. Background information is available in the *Cultural Centre*. Access is via an unpaved road; you can pitch your tent on the *Homestead Campground (short.travel/aus5)* which has a small kiosk. A guided day trip in a 4×4 from Broken Hill can be recommended with *Tri State Safaris (A$230 | tristate. com.au)*. ▥ *G5*

⑩ WHITE CLIFFS

286km / 3 hrs from Broken Hill by car
Opal seekers have turned this area north-east of Broken Hill into a lunar landscape where life is largely spent underground in the cool and shade. After all, temperatures in summer are known to climb above the 40°C mark. See for yourself what it's like to live underground by staying in dug-out accommodation. Imaginatively designed opal jewellery is available from German-born goldsmith Barbara Gasch *(Dugout 142 | tel. 08 80 91 66 34)*. ▥ *G5*

⑪ MUNGO NATIONAL PARK

324km / 5 hrs 45 mins from Broken Hill by car
According to archaeologists, this national park, measuring some 280km², could be one of the cradles of mankind. Archaeological finds bear witness to long-extinct animals and prehistoric human beings. Some fossils are believed to be over 40,000 years old, including the remains of "Mungo Man", one of the oldest evidence of *Homo sapiens*.

The landscape's main attraction is the *Walls of China*, picturesque formations of sand and clay. Some of the roads in this area are dirt tracks in places. For information, including on guided tours and accommodation, *tel. 03 50 21 89 00*. The *Visitor Centre* at the south-west entrance to the park is not always open. ▥ *G6*

A GOOD NIGHT'S SLEEP

A LODGE WITH A WILD SIDE

The prices may be a little steep, but this is a once-in-a-lifetime experience: You'll stay in the safari-inspired *Jamala Wildlife Lodge (8 rooms | 999 Lady Denman Drive | tel. 02 62 87 84 44 | jamalawildlife lodge.com.au | $$$)*, where only a glass wall separates you from the lion or bear sanctuary. Tours of the zoo, meals and drinks are included.

SLEEP UNDER THE STARS

During the day, you share the beach with a bunch of curious kangaroos, at night, with the Milky Way. Unroll your sleeping bag in the open air under the eucalyptus trees at *Mystery Bay Campground (190 Mystery Bay Road | 16km south of Narooma | tel. 04 28 62 23 57 | mysterybaycamp ground.com.au | $)* and let the surf lull you to sleep.

VICTORIA

GOLD, WAVES & APOSTLES

Victoria is Australia in miniature: unlike in most other states, here you'll find (almost) the entire variety of the continent within a few hours' drive.

The multicultural metropolis Melbourne is the heart of the second-smallest federal state and – according to various rankings – one of the best cities to live in in the world. But make sure you go beyond its boundaries: to the Grampians National Park with its ancient rock paintings; to the penguins on Phillip Island and the wombats in

Only eight remain of the Twelve Apostles

Wilsons Promontory National Park; and, of course, to the world's most famous coastal road – the Great Ocean Road.

Victoria has everything: a rugged coastline, endless beaches for surfing, swamps, agricultural land, snow-covered mountains and barren deserts. It was in Victoria that gold was first discovered in 1850. As a result, tens of thousands of people descended on Melbourne to try their luck in the nearby goldfields.

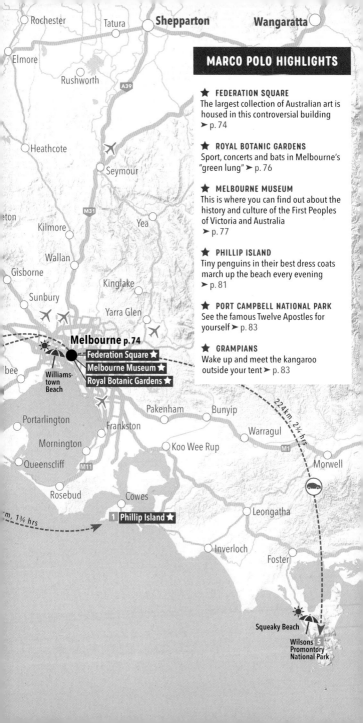

MARCO POLO HIGHLIGHTS

★ **FEDERATION SQUARE**
The largest collection of Australian art is housed in this controversial building ➤ p. 74

★ **ROYAL BOTANIC GARDENS**
Sport, concerts and bats in Melbourne's "green lung" ➤ p. 76

★ **MELBOURNE MUSEUM**
This is where you can find out about the history and culture of the First Peoples of Victoria and Australia ➤ p. 77

★ **PHILLIP ISLAND**
Tiny penguins in their best dress coats march up the beach every evening ➤ p. 81

★ **PORT CAMPBELL NATIONAL PARK**
See the famous Twelve Apostles for yourself ➤ p. 83

★ **GRAMPIANS**
Wake up and meet the kangaroo outside your tent ➤ p. 83

MELBOURNE

(⊞ G7) **What happens when people from 140 nations meet? What sounds in theory like a controversial social experiment is, in reality, a flourishing microcosm. Melbourne (pop. 5 million) celebrates its colourful cultural heritage with more relish than probably anywhere else in the world.**

You can enjoy bratwurst at the local Oktoberfest, halwa during Indian Diwali, and dumplings for Chinese New Year. No wonder the menus in the thousand restaurants offer literally everything, from Mediterranean and Tibetan to Jamaican cuisine. And, although the City of Diversity clings obstinately to traditional customs from all over the world, Melbourne simply is, and always will be, seriously cool and trendy.

Lose yourself in the many alleys

WHERE TO START?

Federation Square is the perfect starting point for visitors as this is where the Information Centre and several interesting museums can be found. Flinders Street Station is on the west side of the square and it's only a short walk across Princes Bridge to the Southbank complex with good restaurants, casino and the Eureka Tower. Whatever you do, don't try to drive into the centre: parking spaces are hard to find, and the car parks are expensive.

and arcades of the city, or enjoy the vast, well-looked-after parks such as the *Royal Botanic Gardens* or *Carlton Gardens*. Getting around is no problem: 🚋 public transport within the square mile of the centre is free. The *City Circle Tram (ptv.vic.gov.au)* runs through the centre every ten minutes daily between 10am and 6pm.

SIGHTSEEING

Make the most of the *Melbourne Greeter Service (Mon–Fri 7.30am–6pm (tel. 03 96 58 96 58); Sat, Sun 9am–6pm (tel. 03 96 58 99 42) | short. travel/aus38)* and book a free 2- to 4-hour 🚋 *city walk* for up to four people. Tours leave daily at 9.30am from Federation Square Visitor Centre.

FEDERATION SQUARE ★ 🐖

Angled façades and crooked corners – this giant, modern museum and restaurant complex on the banks of the Yarra is not only eye-catching, but also an important setting for Melbourne's full-to-bursting calendar of events. The pointed, glazed, zinc-clad building houses the largest holdings of Australian art, including an excellent collection of old and modern Aboriginal art and the National Gallery of Victoria Collection. It is also the perfect spot for watching the world go by (aka people-watching). *Daily 11am–6pm | admission free | fedsq.com | ⏱ 3 hrs*

IMMIGRATION MUSEUM 🏳 🦩

Experience up close how difficult life was for people who came to Australia

here in search of a better life or fleeing from war and persecution. The museum also highlights current immigration issues. *Daily 9am–5pm | A$15 | 400 Flinders Street | museum victoria.com.au/immigrationmuseum | ⊙ 1.5 hrs*

SEALIFE AQUARIUM

You might not spot the leafy sea dragon in its small aquarium straight away. Cool, yes, but not quite the size you might expect a dragon to be; it is almost impossible to distinguish between this little chap and the surrounding marine plants. This is not the case with the sharks, swordfish and rays in the perspex tunnel, where you can experience these sea creatures up close. However, the uncontested stars are without doubt

the king penguins, which slide awkwardly over the ice or roll playfully into the water. *Daily 10am–5.30pm, Sat, Sun until 6pm | A$42, cheaper online | Flinders Street/King Street | melbourneaquarium.com.au | ⊙ 2 hrs*

EUREKA SKYDECK

You won't believe how quickly you'll be whisked to the top of the *Eureka Tower*, the tallest building in Melbourne: it takes only 40 seconds to reach the 88th floor. There are 360-degree panoramic views of the city's skyscrapers and far beyond. If you want to get the adrenaline flowing, then step onto *The Edge (A$12)*, an all-glass cube 300m above the ground. The glass changes from opaque to clear at the touch of a button – a dizzying and surprising effect. *Daily 10am–10pm | from A$23 | Riverside Quay | eurekaskydeck.com. au | ⏱ 1 hr*

DOCKLANDS

A modern suburb has been created at Victoria Harbour on the western side of the city with luxurious architecture of steel and glass. It is as famous for its highly priced apartments as for its popular restaurants, although some are fighting for survival. If you want to settle here, you need to be patient: completion is currently scheduled for 2025.

MELBOURNE STAR OBSERVATION WHEEL

For years, the Ferris wheel on the western side of the city was Melbourne's most famous damp squib. After a lavish opening in 2008, this scandalously expensive steel star revolved for just a few weeks before – in typically Melbourne style – a heatwave literally brought it to a standstill. It took five years to repair. However, you can now once again enjoy the view as you circle above the roofs of Melbourne. The ride is particularly pleasant in the evening. *Sep–Apr 11am–10pm, otherwise until 7pm | from A$27 | Harbour Town | melbournestar.com | ⏱ 30 mins*

ROYAL BOTANIC GARDENS ★ 🐷

The botanic garden on the banks of the Yarra covers more than 35,000m² and is the city's green gem, with lakes, foot and cycle paths, more than 60,000 rare species of plant from all over the world, parrots, flying foxes, nocturnally active possums, shady avenues of trees, sundry theme

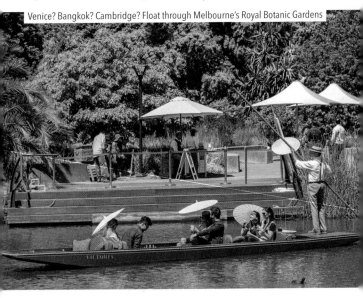
Venice? Bangkok? Cambridge? Float through Melbourne's Royal Botanic Gardens

gardens and elegant tea rooms. In summer, there are open-air performances on the covered *Sidney Myer Music Bowl* stage in the evenings.

The *Aboriginal Heritage Walk (Sun–Fri 11am – duration approx. 90 mins | guided tour A$30 | reservations tel. 03 92 52 24 29)* is a special highlight. Koori guides tells visitors of their history and culture on a stroll around the botanic garden. They explain which plants and types of fruit the Aboriginal people gathered for food or medicine and how they prepared them. *Daily 7.30am until dusk | admission free | Visitors Centre/ Observatory Gate | Birdwood Av. | rbg. vic.gov.au*

INSIDER TIP
Aboriginal Heritage Walk

SHRINE OF REMEMBRANCE

Built to commemorate the Australians who lost their lives in the two World Wars, this temple-like construction is something all schoolchildren visit. Australia in the World Wars? In fact, the fifth continent sent 415,000 soldiers to Europe in World War I, 60,000 of whom fell – a serious figure for a nation that, at the time, had a population of just under 5 million. The masses of visitors inside the shrine can be oppressive, but goes to show how interesting the exhibition on Australia's war history is.

You can head on up to the roof if it's too much, and enjoy the fabulous all-round views beyond the tree tops of the *Royal Botanic Gardens. Daily 10am–5pm, guided tours daily 11am & 2pm | admission free | Kings Domain | Birdwood Av. | shrine.org.au | 1 hr*

MELBOURNE MUSEUM ★

The futuristic, interactive museum combines architecture and the natural environment – you can even walk through a wood in the middle of the museum. The *Bunjilaka Aboriginal Cultural Centre* is an excellent introduction to the spiritual, cultural and political history past and present of Victoria's and Australia's First Peoples. *Daily 9am–5pm | A$15 | Nicholson Street/Carlton Gardens | museum victoria.com.au/melbournemuseum | 1.5 hrs*

ST KILDA

The best-known suburb near the water is like a social-economic résumé of Melbourne. Chic meets shabby, trendy meets retro, elitist meets mainstream. On Acland Street there are designer boutiques next door to second-hand shops, while the fragrance from the vast piles of finest baked goods outside the windows competes with the smell of fish and chips.

Artists and craftspeople offer their wares on the palm-fringed *Esplanade (stkildaesplanademarket.com.au)* on Sundays *(10am–5pm)*. At the end of St Kilda Pier, fresh coffee and snacks are available from the *St Kilda Pier Kiosk*. Or stay for an evening meal at the *Little Blue Restaurant (daily until 5pm; Fri, Sat (also Wed and Thu in summer) until 10pm | littleblue restaurant.com.au | $$–$$$)*. Incidentally, an area behind the kiosk is

Hang out in St Kilda Beach until sunset – it's worth it!

INSIDER TIP
Suburban penguins

home to a colony of little penguins. At sunset from the pier, you can watch them waddle down to their homes under the pier. *stkildamelbourne.com.au*

WILLIAMSTOWN

In this nostalgic port district, the modern city of Melbourne seems miles away and yet it is within eyeshot on the far side of Port Philip. Those interested in history and the romantically inclined should definitely pay a visit. The best way to get there is to take the *Williamstown Ferry (daily from Southgate | A$22 | williamstown ferries.com.au)* across the Yarra River. The 50-minute trip gives you a picture of the old and new dockland areas,

and approaching Williamstown by water is how it would have been seen it in the early 19th century when people arrived on sailing ships. At that time the international port was supposed to have been expanded – but then Melbourne grew in importance.

Many historic buildings line Nelson Place: modest houses have been preserved, as have some of the grander homes, old pubs and imposing civic buildings. These often house small shops or restaurants, which are a welcome stop on any tour. Wind down in summer with a swim on Williamstown Beach. *visitwilliamstown.com.au*

INSIDER TIP
A stylish swimming spot

super bar atmosphere and the popular Toff disco on the second floor. The icing on the cake is the *Rooftop Cinema (A$22 | tel. 03 96 54 53 94 | rooftopcinema.com.au)* which seats 175 (mostly on deckchairs) and has a burger bar, and offers open-air cinema fun from December to early April. *252 Swanston Street | Curtin House | 1st floor | tel. 03 96 63 76 60 | cookie. net.au | $$*

INSIDER TIP
Open-air cinema

RICHMOND OYSTERS
If you like oysters, then this is the place for you. And if you're not so keen on crustaceans, you can order freshly caught fish – in the restaurant or shop. *Closed Sun | 437 Church Street | tel. 03 94 28 51 21 | richmondoysters.com. au | $$*

COLLINGWOOD CHILDREN'S FARM 👥
Every city needs a taste of the country, and city-based nature is certainly a highlight in Melbourne – especially for younger visitors! With meandering meadows and huge, well-kept animal enclosures, this picture-book farm will have kids falling in love with the country life: think petting goats, watching the cows being milked, helping the gardener and riding ponies. *Daily 9.15am–4.45pm | family ticket A$25 | 18 St Heliers Street | Abbotsford | farm.org.au*

RUYI MODERN CHINESE
Take a few hours to enjoy the individual courses of this Chinese speciality restaurant. Ideally, order the five-course menu (there is also a vegetarian option) with the recommended wines. *Closed Sun lunchtime | 16 Liverpool Street | tel. 03 90 90 77 78 | ruyi.com.au | $$$*

SHOPPING

The perfect route for shopping fans: start on *Flinders Street*, opposite *Flinders Street Station*, and head for *Degraves Street*. Cross *Flinders Lane* and on to *Centre Place* (between *Flinders Lane* and *Collins Street*). Cross over *Collins Street (collinsstreet.com.*

EATING & DRINKING

COOKIE
A location with fabulous Thai cuisine, a

au), Melbourne's most elegant shopping mile, and head for the *Block Arcade*, diagonally opposite. It leads you to *Little Collins Street* that is especially interesting between the *Block Arcade* and *Russell Street*. Nearby is the Royal Arcade *(Elizabeth Street/corner of Bourke Street Mall and Elizabeth Street)*, the city's oldest shopping centre.

HARBOUR TOWN MALL
Melbourne's newest shopping complex is in the Docklands on the western end of the city. The best way to get there is with the No. 86 tram for Waterfront City; get off at the Etihad Stadium. Ninety retailers have settled here, many of them with factory outlets. *harbourtownmelbourne.com.au*

MELBOURNE CENTRAL ☂
Shopping centre with some 180 shops, restaurants and boutiques that stock Australian labels such as *RM Williams* (stylish outback fashions). The Central is an architectural work of art: The 50m, brick-built *Shot Tower* (lead shot was produced here between 1888 and 1967) is surrounded by an 84m-high conical glass roof. *Swanston Street/La Trobe Street | melbourne central.com.au*

QUEEN VICTORIA MARKET
Little in youthful Melbourne is as well established as "Vic Market". Since the 1870s, half the city has been congregating here at the weekend to fill its storage cupboards. Souvenirs and clothing are also sold. *Tue, Thu 6am–2pm, Fri 6am–5pm, Sat 6am–3pm, Sun 9am–4pm | qvm.com. au*

SPORT & ACTIVITIES

BIKES FOR RENT 🐷
Melbourne Bike Share (from A$3/day | melbournebikeshare.com.au) provides bikes plus helmets (must be worn!) at a whole range of points around the city.

STAND-UP PADDLING
Have you always fancied giving SUP a go? There's nowhere better to start than off beautiful St Kilda beach with views of the Melbourne skyline? Beginner lessons start daily at 9am and 10.30am *(A$60)* or you can just rent your own board and paddle *(A$30/hr) Pier Road | St Kilda West | supb.com.au*

NIGHTLIFE

Ballet, classical music, theatre and opera are the main features on the programme at the *Arts Centre Melbourne (tickets artscentremelbourne.com.au)*. 🐷 Every evening at 6pm, Tixatsix releases a few A$30 tickets for that evening's performance. Available from the *Box Office (Level 5 | Theatres Building)*.

Melbourne has plenty of variety for night owls. One of the centres is Brunswick Street. You're more likely to find the alternative scene at venues such as *Bar Open (daily | No. 317 | baropen.com.au)* and the *Kodiak Club (Wed–Sun | No. 272 | kodiakclub.com)*. South Yarra, with its trendy bars and

Take a break from shopping in the Block Arcade's cafés

discos, is also popular, especially Chapel Street. At weekends, some parts of *Docklands* are extremely popular. To find out what's happening where, go to *beat.com.au*, the online version of Melbourne's leading street paper.

AROUND MELBOURNE

🟦 PHILLIP ISLAND ⭐
142km / 2 hrs from Melbourne by car

This island south-east of Melbourne is one of the region's most popular destinations for day trips. This is thanks to the little penguins that come out of the water here in the evenings and leisurely retire to their burrows. You can watch them from the visitor seating that has been set up for this purpose *(penguins.org.au)*. Tickets *(from A$26)* and times online or from the *Phillip Island Information Centre (109 Ventnor Road | Summerlands | visitphillipisland.com)*. Another attraction is 🐷 *The Nobbies Centre (admission free)*, on the south-west tip, which has a boardwalk to the coast.

INSIDER TIP
Seal-spotting!

With a little luck you might see some members of Australia's largest seal colony. Interesting boat trips are arranged by *Wildlife Coast Cruises (from A$55 | wildlifecoast cruises.com.au)*. 📖 *G7*

Birdwatching is all part of the Wilsons Promontory experience

2 APOLLO BAY

190km / 3 hrs from Melbourne by car

This pretty fishing village (pop. 1,100) with a 🏖 beach and a diverse hinterland is perfect for a longish stop along the *Great Ocean Road* (see p.166), which, luckily, is how you get there. There are plenty of places to stay right by the beautiful beach, while nearby *Barham River Valley* offers excellent hikes. Modern Australian fare is available at *La Bimba (daily | 125 Great Ocean Road | 1st floor | tel. 03 52 37 74 11 | $$)* – the fresh fish and crayfish especially are unbeatable. 📖 *G7*

3 GREAT OTWAY NATIONAL PARK

205km / 3 hrs 15 mins from Melbourne by car

If you're looking for an earthly setting for a fairy tale, these ancient rainforests (210km to the south-west) with their waterfalls and gigantic eucalyptus trees are just the place. Trees, ferns and bushes wind around each other in their fight for sunlight. Roots hang from high branches, while koalas slumber in the branch forks. On the *Otway Fly Treetop Walk (daily from 9am–5pm | admission A$25 | Beech Forest | otwayfly.com)*, you walk 25m above the ground along the huge trees. Alternatively, you can release your inner Tarzan on the 2½-hour

SIDER TIP
Look out for koalas!

ziplining tour *(A$120).* If you follow the Lighthouse Road to the lighthouse on the cape you're more than likely to spot koalas roaming free. *G7*

⁴ PORT CAMPBELL NATIONAL PARK ★

290km / 4 hrs 30 mins from Melbourne by car along the Great Ocean Road

This narrow nature reserve adjacent to the coast west of Melbourne is home to all the highlights that are familiar to you from the tourist brochures. Conveniently, it's all on the *Great Ocean Road* (see p.166). The *Twelve Apostles* are especially atmospheric early in the morning or in the evening. For an interesting angle of the limestone stacks, go from the car park at the Gibson Steps down the steps to the beach. Not quite so well known, but every bit as spectacular, are formations like *The Grotto* and the *Bay of Martyrs. G7*

⁵ WILSONS PROMONTORY NATIONAL PARK

225km / 3 hrs from Melbourne by car

Wilsons Promontory is in Gippslands, south-east of Melbourne (coast road to New South Wales) and offers a paradise for nature-lovers, hikers and animal observers. Wombats feel very much at home here *(Norman Beach).* The wallabies, possums, emus and koalas that also live here are most active at dusk. Brightly coloured parrots and thousands of waterfowl

live in the eucalyptus forests and swamps in the river estuary, and dolphins, penguins and seals frolic near the white beaches around the peninsula. Here, *Squeaky Beach* really does live up to its name – no special technique is needed to make the sand squeak under your feet. If you've had enough of beach life, there are lovely trails that will lead through the national park. But remember, you're on your own here and food and drink must be brought with you. Find maps and hike information at the *Visitor Centre* in Tidal River or online *(short. travel/aus49). H7*

INSIDER TIP
Noisy sand

GRAMPIANS

(G7) **Just three hours by car from Melbourne, the sandstone ranges (up to 1,000m) of the ★ Grampians rise up out of the green landscape – a paradise for hikers and nature-lovers.**

Brightly coloured parrots screech in the trees, while emus and kangaroos also consider the campsites to be their terrain. And above it all is the glorious deep-blue sky. The mountains, called *Gariwerd* in the local Aboriginal language, are time witnesses to an ancient culture: Aboriginal people lived here for 5,000 years before the Europeans came.

A good starting point is the small town of *Halls Gap* at the north-eastern end of the national park, with a wide

Caves provide shade and shelter in the Grampians

range of accommodation, restaurants and a supermarket.

SIGHTSEEING

BRAMBUK ABORIGINAL CULTURAL CENTRE

The Grampians are also known for their Aboriginal culture. The vegetation here was so plentiful that local indigenous groups had time for artistic and religious pursuits alongside hunting and gathering food. It's no coincidence that the Grampians are home to about 80 per cent of all known Aboriginal rock paintings in Victoria. The imposing cultural centre here holds exhibitions and events to promote this heritage, and the complex also includes the *Gariwerd Dreaming Theatre*, where two short documentaries on local Aboriginal culture are shown. *Daily 9am–5pm | admission free | 277 Grampians Road | brambuk.com.au | ⓘ 1 hr*

EATING & DRINKING

It can get busy here at weekends in the summer, so it's always best to book.

SPIRIT OF PUNJAB

Excellent Indian dishes are served here, many of which are vegetarian. Plus you get to decide how brave – read spicy – you're feeling. *Daily | 161 Grampians Road | tel. 03 53 56 42 34 | spiritofpunjabrestaurant. com | $$*

6pm, Sat & Sun also at lunchtime | 125 Grampians Road | tel. 03 53 56 42 22 | kookaburrahotel.com.au | $$

SPORT & ACTIVITIES

There are more than enough hiking trails and mountain bike tracks here. If you want something quick and easy, then try the much-photographed *Balconies* rock formation. The hike from Wonderland car park to *Pinnacle Lookout* is more challenging, but you'll be rewarded with sensational views – plus the last stretch is through a narrow crevice in the rock. It takes about an hour and a half there and back.

INSIDER TIP
Rocky routes, fabulous views

While the thundering *MacKenzie Falls* undeniably has its charms, that seems to be common knowledge. For a less crowded option, try the *Beehive Falls*, which can be reached in about 30 minutes from the car park of the same name.

KOOKABURRA HOTEL

There's something for everyone here, whether that be pub classics like fish and chips or eye fillet steak, kangaroo fillet or a spinach crêpe. *Tue–Sun from*

A GOOD NIGHT'S SLEEP

DON'T CAMP, GLAMP!

Do you love the wilderness but miss the comforts of home? Try one of the glamping tents at ⚑ *Wilderness Retreats (32 Ring Road | tel. 03 84 27 21 22 | wildernessretreats.com.au | $$$)* near Tidal River in Wilsons Promontory National Park. Make sure to book early as the four permanent tents complete with heating and right at the heart of the national park are snapped up quickly!

CABINS & KANGAROOS

You'll sleep very well in one of the 25 comfortable log cabins with verandas and fabulous views of the mountains at *D'Altons Resort (Glen Street | tel. 03 53 56 46 66 | daltonsresort.com.au | $$)* in the Grampians. Plus, there are animal guests too: every evening, the kangaroos hop into the large garden in search of food – totally unfazed by open-mouthed human visitors.

QUEENSLAND

THE RADIANT SUNSHINE STATE

Snorkelling mask on and let's go! Soft coral reefs sway in the current while a clownfish nibbles on a sizeable mussel. Wait, was that a shark back there?

The ⭐ *Great Barrier Reef*, with its fascinating undersea world, runs for more than 2,300km up the east coast of Australia from Lady Elliot Island to the northernmost tip of Cape York; Queensland's main attraction comprises more than 3,000 individual reefs and over 2,000 tropical islands. But Queensland has much more to offer.

On Mission Beach the rainforest reaches right up to the edge of the sand

There is perfect surfing on the Gold Coast, tranquillity in the mountains inland, a vibrant, subtropical capital – Brisbane – fascinating Aboriginal culture and unspoilt national parks in the adventure region of Cape York.

Queensland *(queensland.com)* is the second largest state in Australia, covering 1.7 million km² (almost seven times the size of the UK), and with a population of less than five million.

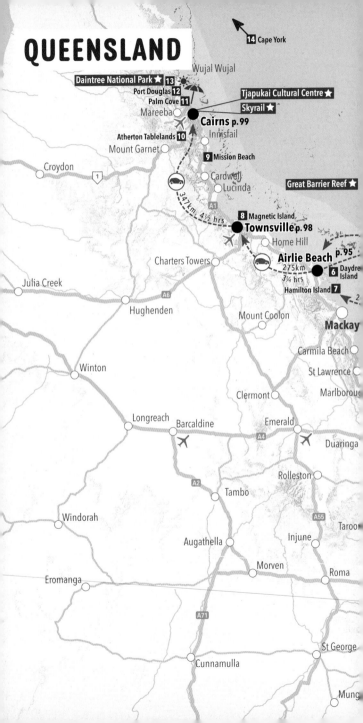

QUEENSLAND

14 Cape York

Wujal Wujal

13 Daintree National Park ★
Port Douglas **12**
Palm Cove **11**
Mareeba

Tjapukai Cultural Centre ★
Skyrail ★

● **Cairns p.99**

Innisfail

Atherton Tablelands **10**
Mount Garnet

9 Mission Beach

Croydon

Cardwell
Lucinda

Great Barrier Reef ★

347 km, 4½ hrs

8 Magnetic Island
● **Townsville p.98**

Home Hill

Charters Towers

Airlie Beach p.95
275 km
3¾ hrs
6 Daydre
Island

Hamilton Island 7

Julia Creek

Hughenden

Mount Coolon

Mackay

Carmila Beach

St Lawrence

Marlborou

Winton

Longreach

Barcaldine

Clermont

Emerald

Duaringa

Rolleston

Tambo

Taroo

Windorah

Augathella

Injune

Morven

Roma

Eromanga

St George

Cunnamulla

Mung

MARCO POLO HIGHLIGHTS

★ **GREAT BARRIER REEF**
The attraction par excellence on the east coast: millions of brightly coloured fish, dolphins, corals and tropical islands ➤ p. 86

★ **BRISBANE**
Pubs with music, world-class restaurants and up-and-coming art – it's all here without any of that big-city hustle and bustle ➤ p. 90

★ **FRASER ISLAND (K'GARI)**
Whales and dolphins swim in the unbelievably blue waters, while dingoes roam the jungle of this huge sand island ➤ p. 94

★ **TJAPUKAI CULTURAL CENTRE**
Culture, history and myths relating to the local Aboriginal people ➤ p. 100

★ **SKYRAIL**
Glide in a cabin over gorges and the canopy of the rainforest ➤ p. 100

★ **DAINTREE NATIONAL PARK**
Tropical rainforests, dream-like beaches and cloud-covered mountains ➤ p. 104

Coral Sea

1095 km, 12½ hrs

Rockhampton
Gladstone
Agnes Water
Ioela
Bundaberg
Fraser Island (K'gari) ★
Hervey Bay   5 Fraser Coast
Maryborough
Gympie   Rainbow Beach   Main Beach
4 Sunshine Coast
Maroochydore
Caloundra
Dalby
Caboolture
woomba   Brisbane ★ p. 90
1 North Stradbroke Island
Ipswich   2 Gold Coast
Lamington National Park 3   Tweed Heads
Warwick
Lismore

200 km
124 mi

BRISBANE

(□□ J5) ★ **Brisbane is like a year-round summer fairy tale: it's almost always T-shirt weather; children splash around in the artificial lagoon, and in the cooler evening hours local bands rock the scene on the rooftop terraces.**

It's hard to imagine that the metropolis owes its existence to a few Conservative British politicians of the early 19th century, who strongly disagreed with liberalisation in New South Wales. They wanted to reinforce transportation to Australia as a "measure of sheer" terror by opening a new penal colony in Moreton Bay. This situation didn't last long, though, and after less than 20 years, the colony was dissolved and Brisbane quickly grew to become a thriving centre, not least thanks to gold being found here in the 20th century.

WHERE TO START?

You can find your way about this city quickly. The real centre is **King George Square**: walk a few yards to **Queen Street Mall** and then on to **Brisbane River**. Cross Victoria Bridge and stroll through the idyllic South Bank Parklands. If you arrive by train, get off at **Roma Street Station**. Buses from all directions stop in the centre. For drivers, multi-storey car parks can be found in the **Myer Centre**, among other places.

With a population of 2.4 million, Brisbane is now the third-biggest city in Australia. Despite that, though, apart from at rush hour, it has little of the usual city hustle and bustle. Queensland's capital not only produces successful musicians – think the Bee Gees and Savage Garden – but also has an excellent pub and restaurant scene.

SIGHTSEEING

QUEENSLAND CULTURAL CENTRE ♥

The colossal concrete complex on the south bank of the river and on both sides of Victoria Bridge in the South Bank Parklands cannot fail to impress with its gallery, museum, library and theatre. The *Queensland Art Gallery (daily 10am–5pm | admission free, excluding special exhibitions | qagoma.qld.gov.au)*, puts on high-quality temporary exhibitions of Aboriginal art and European painting and sculpture. Together with the *Gallery of Modern Art (GoMA)* it is the largest modern art gallery in Australia. The *Queensland Museum (daily 9.30am–5pm | admission free | qm.qld.gov.au)* has rich displays on the history and natural history of Queensland. *arts.qld.gov.au/arts/culturalcentre | ⏱ 1–1.5 hrs each*

SOUTH BANK PARKLANDS

An Australian metropolis without access to the sea – is there any such thing? Yes – but to make up for it, Brisbane simply brought the beach into the city. You can relax on the

BRISBANE

man-made 🐨 *Streets Beach* and the tropical lagoon, or go for a stroll along the *Arbour Path*, which is flanked by brightly coloured flowers – all with views of the city skyline. The view from above is courtesy of the *Wheel of Brisbane (Sun–Thu 10am–10pm, Fri, Sat until 11pm | A$20 | thewheelof brisbane.com.au).* There are many restaurants and food stalls in the vicinity, and you can stroll around a lifestyle market at weekends. *visitsouthbank. com.au*

KOALA SANCTUARY 🚩
No visit to Australia is complete until you have cuddled a koala. And where better to do that than at the world's biggest koala sanctuary? This idyllic animal park, which is also home to kangaroos, Tasmanian devils and other Australian animals, supports numerous animal welfare projects. *Daily 9am–5pm | A$36 | Fig Tree Pocket | Jesmond Road | koala.net | ⊙ 2 hrs*

EATING & DRINKING

Excellent restaurants are to be found at the *Riverside Centre* and *Eagle Street Pier* as well as *Fortitude Valley* and in *New Farm (Merthyr Road/ Brunswick Street). Given Terrace* and *Caxton Street (Paddington)* as well as *Park Road (Milton)* are further recommendations, as is *South Bank.*

ALCHEMY RESTAURANT & BAR
Located on the riverfront, this contemporary restaurant serves top-quality dishes against the backdrop of Story

Bridge and the Brisbane River. *Closed Sun & Sat lunchtimes | 175 Eagle Street | tel. 07 32 29 31 75 | alchemy restaurant.com.au | $$$*

BREAKFAST CREEK HOTEL

This old building, not unlike a country house, is home to a Queensland institution. Excellent beers and the best steaks in the city are served in several bars and restaurants, as well as at what is said to be Brisbane's oldest beer garden. *Daily | 2 Kingsford Smith Drive | tel. 02 32 62 59 88 | breakfast creekhotel.com | $$$*

SHOPPING

The main shopping drag is *Queen Street Mall* with the pleasant *Brisbane Arcade*. Pop in and have a look at

Maiocchi (maiocchi.com.au) – for racks and racks of chic, Australian-designed and made ladies' fashion. *Riverside Market* is worth visiting too *(Sun 8am–3pm, Botanical Garden).*

NIGHTLIFE

A number of good bars and nightclubs can be found in *Fortitude Valley* on *Ann Street*, e.g. *Beat Mega Club (No. 677)* and *GPO Hotel (No. 740)*. Perhaps unsurprisingly in the home of some of Australia's best bands, good live music is also played at, for example, *The Zoo (Wed–Sun | 711 Ann Street)*. The atmosphere is international in the *Down Under Bar (Edward Street | at Central Station below the backpacker hotel)*.

The Riverside Centre is a popular eating and drinking destination

AROUND BRISBANE

➊ NORTH STRADBROKE ISLAND

45km / 1.5 hrs from Brisbane by car and ferry

You've probably heard of Fraser Island, but what about North Stradbroke? "Straddie" is the world's second largest sand island where everything, just like on Fraser Island, grows on sand. If you don't believe us, take a look at the idyllic eucalyptus forests complete with koalas taking a nap in their branch forks! Over in the small town of *Point Lookout*, the name says it all, with incredible ocean views wherever you look. Restaurants, bakeries and a supermarket line the main street.

INSIDER TIP

To walkabout

No trip is complete without a walk to Headland Park at the end of this road – the start of two first-class short walks: the *North* and *South Gorge Walks*. The two walks merge into one another, and you can quite easily walk them in half an hour *(one way)*. But it's worth leaving more time, because kangaroos often jump out on the path – and anyway, this is a view to be savoured. Off the coast you can spot a whale a minute (almost literally) during whale season, and the numerous dolphins and manta rays are an added bonus. Take the *car ferry* to the island *(car incl. 2 adults A$58–78 | stradbrokeferries.com.au)* from Cleveland. *stradbrokeisland.com.* ▥ *J5*

➋ GOLD COAST

78km / 1 hr from Brisbane by car

Hardly any other strip of sand is more of an Australian holiday cliché than this. There are no limits to the pleasure available on the narrow, approximately 70-km-long coastal strip: high-rising luxury hotels, modern apartment blocks, nightclubs, huge shopping malls and casinos compete for the favours of the approximately 12 million visitors who come here every year. The centre is *Surfers Paradise*, a mass of concrete and neon that is not unlike Las Vegas. There are several first-class theme parks in the surrounding area, which you can see in the distance from the *SkyPoint Observation Deck* on the 77th floor of the Q1 Skyscraper *(daily 7.30am–7pm, Fri, Sat until 9pm | A$25 | Hamilton Av. | skypoint.com.au).* Further information at *visitgoldcoast.com.* ▥ *J5*

➌ LAMINGTON NATIONAL PARK

106km / 1.5 hrs from Brisbane by car

Inland from the Gold Coast, this network of paths covering 160km runs through the hilly countryside of the McPherson Range. *O'Reilly's Rainforest Guesthouse (Lamington National Park Road | via Canungra | oreillys.com.au)* organises excellent guided hikes through the rainforest. The 800m *Tree Top Walk* takes you over nine swinging suspension bridges through the rainforest before you get to enjoy the view out over the national park from *Mick's Tower*, 18m above the ground. ▥ *F5*

◳ SUNSHINE COAST

135km / 1 hr 45 mins from Brisbane by car

It does what it says on the tin: dreamy beaches, like the 150-km stretch between Bribie Island and Fraser Island, and pretty resorts. And the sun does almost always shine.

The trip from *Caloundra* to *Noosa Heads (noosaeguide.com)* in the north is well worthwhile. This lovely spot, together with its twin town *Noosaville*, is the touristic heart of the Sunshine Coast (*visitsunshinecoast.com.au*). During the day, people go to the wonderfully wide sheltered beaches such as ✈ *Main Beach, Marcus Beach or Peregian Beach*. Evenings can be spent in the many street cafés and restaurants on Hastings Street. Later you can promenade along the boardwalk under a starry sky. You can go for a short walk in the small *Noosa National Park* close to the city that covers an area of just 4.3km². Remember to look up: there are koalas around.

The rugged sandstone cliff landscape in *Cooloola National Park* to the north can only be explored in a 4×4 (*fourwheeldrive.com.au*), or on a tour, like the one organised by *Great Beach Drive (day tour from A$195 | great beachdrive4wdtours.com)*. Cheap transport links from Brisbane: *tel. 07 54 50 59 33 | airshuttle.com.au | ▥ J5*

◳ FRASER COAST

386km / 3 hrs 30 mins from Brisbane by car

The Fraser Coast, over 300km north of Brisbane, is well known for two reasons. *Hervey Bay* (pronounced "Harvey") is considered by experts to be an excellent place for whale watching. Between August and October there are up to 3,000 humpback whales in the waters off the city. A number of different tours start from *Urangan Boat Harbour*. Information: *Hervey Bay Tourism (Urraween Road/Maryborough Road | discoverhervey bay.com, visitfrasercoast.com)*.

★ *Fraser Island (K'gari)* is also unique in the world: covering 1,840km², it is the largest sand island on earth and became a UNESCO World Heritage Site in 1992. The island is up to 240m high and home to an extraordinary variety of plants and animals. The rainforests and some 40 freshwater lakes can be reached along a sandy track. One of the most beautiful lakes, with a snow-white beach, is *Lake McKenzie*. The island's east coast is the busiest, and the beach can turn into a bit of a motorway. If you've got a bit more time, and some off-road driving experience, venture up to the northwest coast of the island, where an almost untouched natural paradise awaits. *K'gari*, as the Aboriginal people call Fraser Island, can be explored on a well-guided tour or in your own all-terrain vehicle (*permission required | short.travel/aus39*). You can get to the island paradise from Hervey Beach by charter aircraft or ferry. Ferries also go to Fraser Island from ✈ *Rainbow Beach* further south, which has idyllic sand dunes and is much quieter and more relaxed. ▥ J4

INSIDER TIP Solitude in the sand

From Airlie Beach you can access stunning Whitehaven Beach on Whitsunday Island

AIRLIE BEACH

(*III H3*) **The small, lively holiday resort of Airlie Beach (pop. 8,000) is the gateway to the Whitsunday Islands.**

By day, wearing your diving kit or snorkelling goggles, you can jump from the tour boat to explore the colourful world of the coral reefs, or lie back and enjoy the feeling of the sun on your body as you relax in "Airlie's" artificial lagoon. Come the evening, join the "in" crowd and party outdoors at the discos and pubs on the town's only main street, Airlie Beach Road.

EATING & DRINKING

WHITSUNDAY SAILING CLUB
Meet the locals! There are fabulous views of the sea from the large terrace, the food is reliably good and portions generous. *Daily | Airlie Point | tel. 07 49 49 78 94 | $$*

SPORT & ACTIVITIES

CRUISE WHITSUNDAYS
Cruise Whitsundays ferries take you from Airlie Beach to Daydream and Hamilton Islands. There are also organised day trips to the reef with time to snorkel or trips to various islands, such as Whitsunday Island. *Port of Airlie | tel. 07 48 46 70 60 | ww.cruisewhitsundays.com*

Snorkelling is an easy way to experience the colourful underwater world

FLIGHTS OVER THE REEF

Admire the Great Barrier Reef from the air and from the water: after an airborne tour, the Air Whitsunday amphibious aircraft lands directly on the reef and releases its passengers for some snorkelling. Total time: *4½ hrs A$650 | tel. 07 49 46 91 11 | airwhitsunday.com.au*

DIVING 🚿

Many diving schools offer trips and courses over a few days for beginners and experienced divers, for example *Whitsunday Scuba Centre (tours with dive from A$358 | 1/4 Airlie Esplanade | tel. 07 49 46 10 67 | whitsundaydivecentre.com.au).*

AROUND AIRLIE BEACH

Off the coast around Airlie Beach there are 74 tropical islands and lots of islets that make up the Whitsunday Islands (*□ H3*). Only eight of them are inhabited. Some are purely holiday islands with hotel complexes and nightlife, others are protected national parks that can be visited on day trips. Excursion boats can drop the romantically inclined and adventurous off for a night or a few days on some of the many uninhabited islands.

Whitsunday Island, the uninhabited main island, is a particularly attractive national park with mangrove swamps and the snow-white, fine-sandy *Whitehaven Beach*, the most beautiful beach in Queensland. *Hook Island, Long Island, South Molle Island* and *Whitsunday Island* all have campsites where you can stay overnight with a *camping permit*. For useful information and accommodation and tour options go to *tourismwhitsundays.com*

6 DAYDREAM ISLAND

5km / 30 mins from Airlie Beach by ferry

This island seems to have been cut straight out of a catalogue of dream destinations: pure white coral beaches with palms waving in the breeze behind them, flower-filled gardens further inland below rainforest-clad slopes. Not surprisingly, this tiny island – just 1km long and 5km from the mainland – is popular among day-trippers. In March 2017, cyclone "Debbie" caused serious damage on the island, but all his since been repaired. ▯ *H3*

7 HAMILTON ISLAND

20km / 1 hr from Airlie Beach by ferry

The biggest inhabited Whitsunday island also has the best tourist infrastructure – with all the associated advantages and disadvantages. Qantas, Jetstar and Virgin Australia fly direct to the island from Melbourne, Brisbane, Cairns and Sydney. Although the various hotels do cause noticeably more traffic on the beaches, this does not detract from their beauty. There are regular ferries from Hamilton to

SUICIDE IN THE REEF

The Great Barrier Reef is *the* visitor attraction in Queensland, and every day numerous boats bring tourists to its beautiful diving and snorkelling areas. The question is, for how much longer?

Rising water temperatures are causing difficulties for the corals, that are slowly but surely releasing a deadly stress reaction. The colourful algae that live on the corals and are responsible for the stunning colours are being rejected by their hosts. It is effectively suicide because the corals will not be able to survive without the algae. In 2016, the reef experienced the worst coral bleaching to date, and in some areas up to 95% of the corals died. The extent of the disaster wrought by cyclone "Debbie" in 2017 has yet to be fully established.

You can help preserve this natural miracle by learning more before your visit by going to the website of the Australian Government's Great Barrier Reef Marine Park Authority *(short. travel/aus40)* and observing the rules of behaviour. You can also become involved in projects such as "Eye on the Reef" or the "Marine Discovery Program" *(short.travel/aus42)*.

Daytrippers miss the idyllic evening atmosphere on Magnetic Island

Airlie Beach, or you can join a day trip to the reef or Whitehaven Beach. *hamiltonisland.com.au.* ⌑ *H3*

TOWNSVILLE

(⌑ *H3*) **You might not instantly be bowled over by this busy harbour town (pop. 180,000) halfway between Airlie Beach and Cairns.**

But don't reject it too hastily, because the attractive promenade *The Strand* with lots of restaurants and beach sections (with jellyfish nets) is perfect for relaxing. From the granite rock *Castle Hill* you can see all the way to interesting Magnetic Island, which is well worth a visit

REEF HQ

The fascinating display of the under-sea world around the *Great Barrier Reef* should not be missed. *Daily 9.30am–5pm | A$28 | 2 Flinders Street | reefhg.com.au | ⊙ 2 hrs*

THE WATERMARK

Café and restaurant in trendy, cool design with modern Australian cuisine with views out over both park and sea. *Daily | 72 The Strand | tel. 07 47 72 42 81 | watermarktownsville. com.au | $$*

AROUND TOWNSVILLE

8 MAGNETIC ISLAND

8km / 25 mins from Townsville by ferry

This holiday island with lovely beaches and a much slower pace is a popular destination for day trippers. Drive to pretty Horseshoe Bay to the north of the island, where a jellyfish net guarantees safe bathing. Ferries depart from Breakwater Terminal: *Sealink (return approx. A$33 | sea linkqld.com.au). visitmagneticisland. com.au | ⊞ H3*

CAIRNS

(⊞ H2) **The picturesque town of Cairns in the north (pop. 160,000) is the perfect starting point for boat trips to the Great Barrier Reef, hikes through the tropical rainforest and excursions to the northernmost point of Cape York.**

It's instantly obvious that Cairns lives and breathes mass tourism. But then, how could it be otherwise, with the world's biggest coral reef right at the front door, the brightly coloured underwater world of the Great Barrier Reef? Cairns is at its busiest on the picturesque *Esplanade*, where you can cool down in the man-made bathing lagoon, enjoy a huge ice cream and work your way through the offers of the various souvenir shops. And when

the sun sinks behind the tableland, the numerous pubs and restaurants come to life. There's also always something going on along the beach promenade, where information panels impart the city's history as you walk by.

SIGHTSEEING

CAIRNS MUSEUM

Cairns looks back on a rather unusual history. In just two centuries, a once-pristine coastline transformed into a coveted gold rush hotspot and tourist magnet. Travel through the city's history for yourself here in the museum. *Mon–Sat 10am–4pm | A$10 | Lake Street, Ecke Shields Street | cairnsmuseum.org.au | ⊙ 1 hr*

CAIRNS AQUARIUM 😋

A reef you can walk through. The aquarium has offered young and old alike a bright and fun learning environment dedicated to the reef and the tropics ever since it opened its doors in late 2017. Make sure you

WHERE TO START?

The **esplanade** in the city centre is bursting with life. You'll find all sorts of eateries, hotels, the lagoon for an inviting swim and streets of shops around the corner. The harbour with boat tours to the Great Barrier Reef is just a short walk away. From the railway station it's about 15 minutes on foot; from the airport just a 10-minute drive by taxi or shuttle bus.

Grab dinner at Cairns' Night Market before you do some shopping

check the programme online before you go so you don't miss the presentation every half hour. *Daily 9am–5pm | A$46, children A$28 | Lake Street, Ecke Florence Street | cairnsaquarium.com. au | ⏱ 2 hrs*

FLECKER BOTANIC GARDENS 🐾

The more than 100 different species of palm tree, orchids and climbers will immerse you in the variety of tropical plants that grow here. At the *Aboriginal Plant Use Garden*, you can learn about plants that indigenous Australians grew thousands of years ago for food or medicine. The gardens are so vast that you can easily spend a whole morning here. *Mon–Fri 7.30am–5.30pm, Sat, Sun 8.30am–5.30pm | admission free | Collins Av.*

TJAPUKAI CULTURAL CENTRE ★

The *Aboriginal Cultural Park* next to the *Skyrail* base station is run by local Aboriginal groups. The tour through the park includes an introduction to the indigenous Australians' world of myths and a film on the history of the Aboriginal people since the arrival of the white settlers. There's also a visit to a museum, a dance show, a demonstration of the didgeridoo and of how to throw a spear and a boomerang. Evening events are also programmed. *Daily | from A$62 | reservations, tel. 07 40 42 99 99 | tjapukai.com.au | ⏱ 2 hrs*

SKYRAIL ★

The 7.5-km-long cable car takes you into the mountainous countryside with its fascinating vegetation inland from Cairns. The cabins glide over the valleys and provide views of the waterfalls on *Barron River* too. Explanations on the flora and fauna of the rainforest can be found at two stopping points where you can break your trip en route. The destination is *Kuranda*, once an alternative lifestyle hippie settlement, now a teeming souvenir market. The best way to return is on the *Kuranda Scenic Railway (ksr.com.au)* that makes an adventurous and twisty descent back down to the plain. *Round trip A$113 | from Smithfield Terminal | skyrail.com.au*

EATING & DRINKING

OCHRE RESTAURANT �

Aboriginal recipes and ingredients are the attraction of this unusual restaurant. *Daily | 6/1 Marlin Parade | tel. 07 40 51 01 00 | ochrerestaurant.com. au | $$$*

SHOPPING

You'll find souvenirs at the *Night Market* held every evening on the esplanade, and mainly Asian food to quell your hunger. Don't miss the colourful *Rusty's Market (Fri, Sat until 6pm, Sun until 3pm | Grafton Street)*, where you can work your way through the variety of exotic fruit.

SPORT & ACTIVITIES

DIVING

Diversion Dive Travel (20 mins north in Palm Cove | tel. 07 40 39 02 00 | short. travel/aus11) organises trips lasting one or several days in fast boats to the reef – with diving instruction from A$300.

ESPLANADE SWIMMING LAGOON 🐖

Just a few yards from the town centre you can cool off in this well-cared-for bathing area with a view of the ocean. What more could you want – especially as it's all free! Come early in the afternoon to secure one of the barbecue spots on the grass for a barbecue party.

EXCURSIONS & CRUISES TO THE REEF

Day trips are organised from Cairns to the Outer Reef *(A$215–250)*, e.g. by *Sunlover Reef Cruises (tel. 07 40*

DREAMTIME

Dreamtime is the English name for the creation myths of indigenous Australians. The ancient cultures of Australia's First Peoples are based exclusively on oral traditions. Many of the legends tell of the time when everything began: landscapes, animals and mankind. The protagonists in the mythology are spirits that continue to influence life. Aboriginal Australians believe they are closely linked to these spirits, and that they are everywhere in nature.

50 13 33 | sunlover.com.au) or a visit to the small coral Green Island by *Great Adventures (tel. 07 40 44 99 44 | greatadventures.com.au)*. You'll be able to snorkel on either tour, but if you want to dive, then take the tour to the Outer Reef.

HELICOPTER FLIGHT

What a treat: a scenic helicopter tour of the Barrier Reef with fabulous views and opportunities to take unbeatable photos and videos from the air. Flights lasting 30 or 45 minutes from A$400 per person with *GBR Helicopters (gbrhelicopters.com.au)*.

AROUND CAIRNS

⑨ MISSION BEACH

129km / 2 hrs from Cairns by car
As beach holidays north of Cairns have become very expensive, places such as Mission Beach are popular, especially among the younger crowd. Mission Beach is a good place to start a hiking or diving tour *(divethereef. com)*. Day trips to *Dunk Island (dunk-island.com)* are also possible. Covered in rainforest, it also has a camping site and café. Just 50km north of Mission Beach, check out *Paronella Park (daily 9am–7.30pm | A$46 | Mena Creek | paronellapark. com.au)*, where a hopeless romantic has built a fairy-tale castle in the tropical parkland. *missionbeachtourism. com.* 🗺 H2

⑩ ATHERTON TABLELANDS

68km / 1 hr 15 mins from Cairns by car
Mountains of volcanic origin covered with dense vegetation tower up 900m west of Cairns. Fascinating ecological niches have evolved in ancient craters, around deep lakes and spectacular waterfalls, and are home to a host of tropical birds and rare animals. One of the loveliest spots is the enigmatic *Mount Hypipamee*, the geological origins of which have yet to be explained. There are wonderful waterfalls with crystal-clear waterholes everywhere in the Tablelands. Four of the most beautiful can be reached on the 15-km *Waterfall Circuit* from *Millaa Millaa*. Don't forget your togs!

You can bathe beneath beautiful waterfalls in the Atherton Tablelands

The little historical town *Yungaburra* (pop. 1,100), that is largely a conservation area, is a great place to start. There are several good restaurants in Yungaburra, such as *Nick's Swiss-Italian Restaurant (Tue–Sun in the evening, Sat, Sun also at lunchtime | 33 Gillies Highway | tel. 07 40 95 33 30 | $$)*, and also antique shops. An authentic market is held in the town every fourth Sunday of the month. *athertontableland.com.au.* *H2*

11 PALM COVE 🌴

30km / 30 mins from Cairns by car

Of all the beach sections to the north of Cairns, Palm Cove is without doubt the most elegant. Luxury resort hotels, cafés and restaurants line the 1.5-km-long promenade next to the pristine palm beach. A net in front of the beach protects visitors from jellyfish, mean-

INSIDER TIP
Sting-free swimming

ing a swim is on the cards. Fun fact: The striking, thick-stemmed melaleuca trees along the road are strictly protected and may only be pruned by the authorities, even on private property. Furthermore, no building can be taller than the nearest melaleuca tree! *H2*

12 PORT DOUGLAS

68km / 1 hr from Cairns by car

The *Captain Cook Highway* is a superb panoramic route running along the

Rock art tours in the company of a Nugal-warra Elder are available from Cooktown

coast to Port Douglas (pop. 3,500), 70km north of Cairns. Until the end of the 1980s, this was a modest little village; it has now been transformed into a sophisticated holiday resort with generally excellent hotels and restaurants that charge correspondingly high prices *(tourismportdouglas. com.au | visitportdouglasdaintree. com.au).*

Four Mile Beach is an immaculate stretch of beach that starts at the end of *Macrossan Street*, the main road of shops. Climb the stairs at the south-eastern end to reach the look-out point – we promise the view is worth every bead of sweat! Every morning, at least a dozen sailing boats and catamarans set off for the Great Barrier Reef. Boats operated by *Quicksilver (from A$250 | tel. 07 40 87 21 00 | quicksilver-cruises.com)*

moor about 90 minutes later at a pontoon on the Outer Reef, from where diving and snorkelling tours start. *H2*

🔟 DAINTREE NATIONAL PARK ⭐
141km / 2 hrs 45 mins from Cairns by car

The protests of committed environmentalists have resulted in Australia's most important and beautiful tropical rainforest being saved from the axe. Today, the breathtaking Daintree National Park, north of Cairns, is a protected area and a UNESCO World Heritage Site. Ancient giant trees, lianas, ferns, palms and moss give way to mangrove forests near the sea. One of the world's largest birds, the flightless cassowary, lives in this fantastic wilderness. Sadly, sightings in the wild are rare as this bird is as shy as it is incredibly fast. Saltwater crocodiles can be seen in the two largest rivers in the national park. Boat trips on *Daintree River*, hikes in *Mossman Gorge (best with a local guide | A$75/90 mins | mossman gorge.com.au)* and at dream-like *Cape Tribulation* give a good impression of the fragile beauty of this tropical landscape. The road is surfaced as far as Cape Tribulation (a worthwhile destination for a day tour from Cairns or Port Douglas). However, it is narrow in places and leads through the middle of the rainforest.

Daintree is of great spiritual significance to the local Kuku Yalanji people.

INSIDER TIP
Traditional fishing

Along the *Bama Way* between Daintree River and Cooktown, local people let you gain an insight into their everyday life by going fishing, for example. A range of one- to two-day tours are available *(Adventure North Australia | from A$255 | tel. 07 40 28 33 76 | adventurenorthaustralia.com)*. 🕮 H2

🔟 CAPE YORK

817km / 18 hrs from Cairns by car

Cape York is a destination for those with a real thirst for adventure. The northernmost point in Australia, enclosed on three sides by the sea, is larger than England but home to only about 10,000 inhabitants, most of whom live in their own territorial areas or settlements. Large areas of Cape York remain unexplored. Savannahs with termite hills several feet high, light-filled eucalyptus forests and rainforest with prolific vegetation. One solitary road leads from Cairns to the end of the continent, known as *The Tip* or *Pajinka*. The 974-km-long stretch is largely a dust track and only drivable in the dry season between May and October. Petrol and simple places to stay can be found in roadhouses or stations along the route. You should plan five or six days for one stretch. Guided trips are offered by tour operators in Cairns, including *Heritage Tours (e.g. 10 days with a return flight to Cairns and stay in a tent A$2,900 | heritagetours.com.au)*. 🕮 G1

A GOOD NIGHT'S SLEEP

LUXURY IN THE WILD

Kingfisher Bay Resort (262 rooms | tel. 07 41 20 33 33 | kingfisherbay.com | $$$) on Fraser Island's west coast is so much more than just a place to rest your head. The huge resort complete with pool blends so idyllically into the landscape you'll start to feel like part of nature yourself.

MILLENNIA-OLD WELLNESS

Pure relaxation at the heart of the rainforest. The beautiful *Daintree Eco Lodge & Spa (Mossman Daintree Road | tel. 07 47 77 73 77 | daintree-ecolodge.com.au | $$$)* offers 15 luxurious villas and an extensive spa that incorporates ancient, natural Aboriginal treatments.

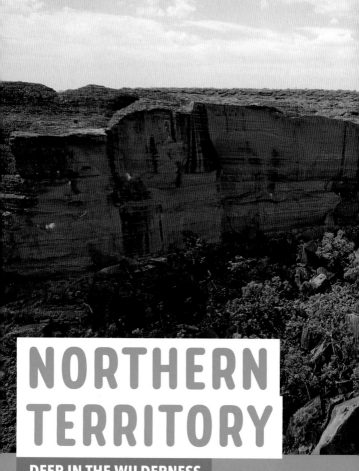

NORTHERN TERRITORY

DEEP IN THE WILDERNESS

When you hear the name "Australia", do you yearn for vast and dramatic landscapes, rich in ancient cultures and traditions? If so, then the Northern Territory is the place for you.

You'll gain deep insights into humanity's oldest culture in the fabulous national parks of the tropical north, such as the Kakadu and Litchfield national parks. Some of the world's oldest rock paintings are tucked away here too. South of Alice Springs, Uluru – a

Kings Canyon is the main attraction in Watarrka National Park

sacred place for the people of this region – rises up out of the never-ending desert, exerting a mystic pull for tourists from all over the world.

Meanwhile, the other attractions of the Red Centre, such as the rugged mountain chain of the MacDonnell Ranges, impressive Kings Canyon and the unmistakeable rocks of Kata Tjuta, are all worth the long journey.

NORTHERN TERRITORY

Timor Sea

INDIAN OCEAN

354 km, 3¾ hrs

Kunur

Broome

Derby

Fitzroy Crossing

Billiluna

Balgo

MARCO POLO HIGHLIGHTS

★ **LITCHFIELD NATIONAL PARK**
Croc-free swimming in picture-perfect natural pools at the heart of the rainforest ➤ p. 114

★ **KAKADU NATIONAL PARK**
Crocodiles, termite mounds and encounters with mankind's oldest culture ➤ p. 114

★ **KATHERINE GORGE**
Canoe your way through the breathtaking gorge ➤ p. 116

★ **KINGS CANYON (WATARRKA)**
Hike through a million-year-old gorge ➤ p. 118

★ **ULURU–KATA TJUTA NATIONAL PARK**
A red monolith and 36 mysterious "heads" ➤ p. 119

3 Tiwi Islands

Milingimbi

Nhulunbuy

155 km · 1¾ hrs

Darwin
p. 110

1 Territory Wildlife Park

Jabiru

Arnhemland 4

Batchelor

Kakadu National Park ★
p. 114

gul

2 Litchfield National Park ★

Alyangula

Bulman

adeye

Pine Creek

5 Nitmiluk National
Park

24

Numbulwar

Katherine
p. 116

20

Katherine Gorge ★

Ngukurr

1

80

1210 km · 13½ hrs

96

Daguragu

Elliott

AUSTRALIA

87

Tennant Creek

66

Canteen Creek

Willowra

Nyirripi

5

Haasts Bluff

Alice Springs
p. 117

Hermannsburg 6

7 Kings Canyon (Watarrka) ★

87

450 km · 5¼ hrs

Yulara

8 Uluru-Kata Tjuta National Park ★

200 km
124 mi

DARWIN

(□ D1) **For a long time, it was said that only those fond of digesting flies and chugging pints of beer could find a home in the capital city of the Northern Territory.**

In fact, Darwin (pop. 140,000) has long since brushed off the desert dust to welcome visitors who come to explore its impressive and inviting harbour district, large well-maintained parks and remarkable gastronomy. Try out the food at the waterfront or, even better, at Mindil Beach Sunset Market. The weather, however, is not to everyone's taste: it's either hot and bone dry (May–October) or hot and sticky (the rest of the year).

In any case, most people don't choose Darwin for Darwin itself, but as a base to explore the splendour of the surrounding national parks: Litchfield first and foremast and then, of course, Kakadu National Park.

WHERE TO START?

At the lower end of **Mitchell Street** you'll find yourself in the thick of things. Highway 1 leads into the city. Parking in the centre is no problem. If you're travelling by train, the station is 15km from the city centre (Berrimah Road) and you have to take a shuttle bus or taxi. The same applies for travellers who arrive at the airport, which is 12km away.

SIGHTSEEING

WATERFRONT

The newly designed harbour is the cherry on the cake that is modern Darwin. There are two palm-fringed lagoons where you can cool down – ☛ *Recreation Lagoon*, free entry, is surrounded by cafés, restaurants and boutiques. Make yourself at home at, for instance, the *Coffee Club (daily | 7 Kitchener Drive | tel. 08 89 41 04 22 | coffeeclub.com.au | $–$$)*, where you can enjoy a wonderful breakfast or lunch until 5pm.

AQUASCENE FISH FEEDING 🎎

Every day at high tide, fish come close to the shoreline at Doctor's Gully to be fed. It's an excellent opportunity to see catfish, mullet and rays up close. *A$15, children A$10 | 28 Doctors Gully Road | aquascene.com.au | ⊘1–2 hrs*

BOTANIC GARDENS ☛

In 1870, the gardener Maurice Holtz laid out Darwin's magnificent botanic park. The gardens contain more than 400 species of palm tree that partly grow in a miniature rainforest, a small orchid nursery and an artificial waterfall and swamps. Covering 42,000m², it is one of the botanic gardens with the greatest variety of species in the southern hemisphere. *Daily 7am–7pm | admission free | Gilruth Av./Gardens Road | short.travel/aus16*

MUSEUM & ART GALLERY OF THE NORTHERN TERRITORY

The museum provides a very good insight into the culture and natural

Relax on Darwin's waterfront, complete with bathing lagoon

history of the Northern Territory and has an interesting collection of regional art dating back up to 46,000 years. How many art museums can compete with that?

Back in 1974, Cyclone Tracy swept through Darwin at Christmas, razing the city virtually to the ground. Experience the acoustic force of the hurricane in the darkroom. The *Darwin Ski Club*, opposite, has an excellent beer garden. *Mon–Fri 9am–5pm, Sat & Sun 10am–5pm | admission free | Conacher Street | Fannie Bay | magnt.net.au | ◷ 1–2 hrs*

INSIDER TIP
Cyclone experience

EATING & DRINKING

As well as in the harbour quarter, you will find lots of restaurants on *Mitchell Street* and at *Cullen Bay Marina*.

MY FRIEND'S KITCHEN 🐖

This unassuming street café at the heart of Darwin cooks up noodle soups, amazing spring rolls and a whole range of other Vietnamese dishes. *Daily, Sat & Sun evening only | 52 Mitchell Street | tel. 08 89 81 89 81 | $*

PEE WEE'S

Here, under palm trees and with a great view of Fannie Bay, you can indulge in creative Australian food and good wines. *Tue–Sat from 4pm | Alec Fong Lim Drive | East Point | tel. 08 89 81 68 68 | peewees.com.au | $$$*

SHOPPING

Darwin is well known for its many markets, e.g. the *Parap Village Markets (Sat 8am–2pm | Parap Road)*, the *Mindil Beach Sunset Market (see p. 112)* and the *Rapid Creek Market (Sat,*

Sun 6.30am–1.30pm | Rapid Creek Business Village | 48 Trower Road | approx. 20 mins from the city). The Territory's culture pearls are available from *Paspaley Pearls (Bennett Street/Smith Street Mall)*. The best address for freshly caught fish is *Frances Bay:* At *Mr Barra (shop 20 | mrbarra.com.au)* behind Fisherman's Wharf and in *Darwin Fish Market (shop 5 | access via Frances Bay Drive | darwinfishmarket.com)*, the seafood and shellfish displays will make your mouth water.

Mason Gallery (7/21 Cavenagh Street | masongallery.com.au) is one of Darwin's best art galleries. 🐖 *Readback Book Exchange (32 Smith Street Mall)* sells certified pieces by Aboriginal artists at lower prices. Note: if shipping to Europe, works of art are subject to tax based on their value!

SPORT & ACTIVITIES

EAST POINT RESERVE

The park on the beach close to the city centre is a popular place for picnics and relaxing and for swimming in Lake Alexander – a saltwater basin that is free of stinger jellyfish all year round. During the rainy season, the lake is sometimes closed if the bacteria levels get too high.

CROCODILE CRUISE 👹

While you might be interested in seeing some of the Northern Territory's most fascinating inhabitants, a surprise meeting is probably not the best way! Put your mind at rest with a 1-hour tour on the Adelaide River. Tours run several times a day and provide a chance to get up close and personal with the reptiles. *A$45, children A$30, families A$125 | jumpingcrocodile.com.au*

BEACHES

MINDIL BEACH

The quickest way to make friends back home envious: send them a picture of the tropical sun sinking into the sea on Mindil Beach, which is only a 20-minute walk from the city. Alternatively, take the minibus *(A$5)*. On Thursdays, the legendary sunset is celebrated at the 🐦 *Mindil Beach Sunset Market (April–Oct 5–10pm | mindil.com.au)* with reasonably priced food stands, fine arts and crafts, street performers and the sounds of the didgeridoo.

WATCH OUT – CROC ABOUT!

Salties is the almost affectionate nickname for the saltwater crocodiles, which not only live in large numbers along the coasts in the far north of Australia, but also feel completely at home in the *billabongs* (waterholes) of the national parks. As you are certain to come off worse in an encounter with one of these sharp-toothed saurians, please do not ignore this absolute rule:

"Only bathe where it is explicitly permitted."

Barramundi versus saltwater crocodile

NIGHTLIFE

DECKCHAIR CINEMA

Darwin really comes to life once the sun has disappeared over the horizon. The open-air cinema runs from April to November and has 250 deckchairs and 100 seats. Food and drinks are available (incl. beer and wine) but be sure to take good insect protection with you. *Daily performances 7.30pm, Sat, Sun also 9.30pm | Jervois Road | Waterfront | deckchaircinema.com.au*

SUNSET CRUISE

With such wonderful sunsets, an atmospheric boat trip in the late afternoon around the extensive harbour bay is a good idea. Perhaps combine it with a delicious dinner on board the nostalgic schooner Alfred Nobel. This will be accompanied by good wine, a refreshing breeze and wonderful views of the tropical coastline. Booking at *Darwin Harbour Cruises (daily at sunset | A$58 | from Stokes Wharf | tel. 08 89 42 31 31 | darwinharbourcruises. com.au).*

AROUND DARWIN

1 TERRITORY WILDLIFE PARK 👥
50km / 40 mins from Darwin by car
This large park provides a very good insight into the fauna and flora of the Northern Territory and allows you to get up close and personal with the park's animal inhabitants. Demonstrations (with birds of prey, for example) take place multiple times a day. *Daily 9am–5pm | A$32, children A$16 | Berry Springs | territory wildlifepark.com.au | ⏱ 3 hrs | 🗺 D1*

2 LITCHFIELD NATIONAL PARK ★

122km / 1 hr 30 mins from Darwin by car

This national park is a wild oasis with waterfalls, gorges, rainforest and huge termite mounds. You can swim in a number of waterholes without having to worry about crocodiles. The *Wangi Falls* and *Florence Falls* are particularly beautiful – and are great for swimming. There are several simple campsites in the vicinity.

If there's a creature that knows a thing or two about building, it's the compass termite; check out the *Magnetic Termite Mounds*, just outside the small town of Bachelor. The impressive structures look like tombstones against the landscape. *Admission free | short.travel/aus50 |* ☐ *D1*

3 TIWI ISLANDS

80km / 2 hrs 30 mins from Darwin by ferry

Off the coast of Darwin are *Melville* and *Bathurst*, two islands whose inhabitants have retained their own distinct culture and are well known for their craftwork and painting. Tourism is carefully regulated. The one-a-day boat trip goes to Bathurst, the main island, where you'll be able to meet the local residents. Bookings through *Sealink (day tour from A$295 | sealinknt.com.au).* ☐ *D–E1*

KAKADU NATIONAL PARK

(☐ *E1*) ★ ⚑ **Kakadu National Park is an important site for local Aboriginal people who have called this land home for tens of thousands of years.**

Over 5,000 ancient rock painting are hidden here, some accessible to tourists. Potentially Australia's most famous national park, Kakadu is located 255km east of Darwin in the western part of the Arnhem Land Escarpment, that runs 500km from north to south, separating it from the region of Arnhem Land in the east.

The almost 20,000km² Unesco World Heritage Site can be reached along the surfaced Arnhem Highway in a conventional car. The main centre of the park is *Jabiru*, where you can find places to stay that will suit every wallet. The best time to go is during the dry season (May–October) and allow at least two to three days. *Pass A$25 per person/valid for 14 days, available from the Visitor Centre*

SIGHTSEEING

BOWALI VISITOR CENTRE

The tourist information centre just outside Jabiru is the first port of call for the national park. It contains a good exhibition on the history of the region, in parts related by local people, as well as maps and other aids to orientation.

It also issues the obligatory park pass. *Tel. 08 89 38 11 21 | parksaustralia. gov.au/kakadu |* ⏱ *1 hr*

ROCK PAINTINGS

He's been lying there like that, naked and with his legs apart, for thousands of years. "X-ray man" is one of the best-known rock paintings; some 250,000 visitors admire him every year on the short walk to *Nourlangie Rock (daily from 8am until sunset)*. It's much quieter at the no less impressive rock paintings of *Ubirr* on the East Alligator River. A circular walk leads up to a 250-m-high plateau that offers wonderful views of the alluvial land.

IDER TIP
Rock art without the crowds

YELLOW WATER BILLABONG

A boat trip across the Yellow River at sunrise or sunset against the backdrop of the twittering of countless birds, is like a massage for the soul … until the idyll is rudely interrupted by a snapping crocodile that suddenly appears beside the boat – phew! *Bookable from Cooinda Lodge | A\$90 | tel. 08 89 79 01 45 | short.travel/aus18*

Be sure to visit the nearby 🦎 *Warradjan Aboriginal Cultural Centre (daily 9am 5pm | admission free)* dedicated to local Aboriginal culture.

JIM JIM FALLS & TWIN FALLS

We recommend an all-terrain vehicle for this 70-km detour from Kakadu Highway – and it's only possible during the dry season. The attractions include the *Jim Jim Falls*, which are over 200m high, and a little boat trip *(A\$13)* to the *Twin Falls*. Having said that, from about June the Jim-Jim waterfalls dwindle to little more than a trickle. One alternative during the rainy season is an hour-long sightseeing flight from Jabiru *(A\$250)* with *Kakadu Air (kakaduair.com.au)*.

Florence Falls serve as a natural bathing spot

Spectacular Katherine Gorge

Heritage Tour (kakaduculturaltours. com.au). 📖 E2

KATHERINE

(📖 E2–3) **Whichever direction you are arriving from, the little town of Katherine (pop. 10,000) will initially feel like a metropolitan city.**

So, brush off the dust of the outback, refuel the car, and then admire the tremendous array of food in the supermarket. And if, after a few days, you feel drawn back to the landscape of the Northern Territory, drive through the Nitmiluk National Park with the Edith Falls and spectacular Katherine Gorge.

AROUND KAKADU NATIONAL PARK

🔲 ARNHEM LAND

Trips to Arnhem Land, a largely under-explored area and one of the final frontiers for mass tourism, are well worthwhile. The Yolngu and other First Peoples have native title rights to much of Arnhem Land. For cultural reasons, access is granted to only a small number of visitors. Tours and information: Arnhemlander Cultural &

AROUND KATHERINE

🔳 NITMILUK NATIONAL PARK
28km / 30 mins from Katherine by car
Katherine River has spent millions of years burrowing its way through the sandstone plateau, forming a system of 13 gorges in total: the ★ *Katherine Gorge* (28km), which reveals its magic quite spectacularly when the sun hangs low in the sky. Hire a canoe *(Nitmiluk Tours | single canoe A$81, double canoe A$139 | tel. 08 89 71 08 77 | nitmiluktours.com.au)* or walk the *Baruwei Loop Walk* to the lookout platform (approx. 1.5 hours).

Real fans of the outdoor life would do well to hire the canoe for two days (*single canoe A$167, double canoe A$244*) to give themselves enough time to paddle to the sixth or seventh gorge. As well as campsites, there are also several chalets available to rent.

The *Edith Falls* are also well worth the detour from Stuart Highway. They cascade into a pool surrounded by palm trees, where swimming is delightful. Now and then, you can join a tour with the ranger and there is also a lovely campsite and a small kiosk. *E1*

INSIDER TIP
Swim under palm trees

ALICE SPRINGS

(*E4*) **It isn't possible for anyone to choose a more remote spot for a town: "The Alice" – as the approx. 25,000 residents call it – is about 1,500km from both Darwin and Adelaide, and almost 3,000km from Sydney.**

The town was established in 1872 as a telegraph station to connect Port Augusta and Darwin. Today, the station is an open-air museum that is well worth a visit, but most of the more than 500,000 tourists who come to Alice Springs every year are drawn straight on to the breathtaking landscape of the Red Centre.

SIGHTSEEING

ANZAC HILL

From here you have a good view over the city. The MacDonnell Ranges in the background turn a wonderful red at sunrise and sunset.

ROYAL FLYING DOCTOR SERVICE

A birth in the bush? An emergency in an outback community? How can medical assistance be given if you're 1,000km from the nearest hospital? Find out here. And incidentally, your admission charge is an important source of income for the Flying Doctor Service. *Daily 9am–4pm | A$17 | 8–10 Stuart Terrace | rfdalicesprings.com.au | 1.5 hrs*

SCHOOL OF THE AIR

There's a lot of space in the world's largest classroom: 1.3 million km². Children in the outback get their lessons from hundreds of miles away now in their own living rooms via the internet. Watch through a glass wall and hear through speakers what the teacher is telling his distant students. *Mon–Sat 8.30am–4.30pm, Sun from 1.30pm | A$10 | 80 Head Street | assoa.nt.edu.au | 1 hr*

TELEGRAPH STATION

This lovingly renovated telegraph station, built of hewn rock in 1872, takes you back to Australia's pioneering days. The entry fee includes a guided tour. *Daily 9am–5pm | A$15 | North Stuart Highway | alicesprings telegraphstation.com.au | 1–1.5 hrs*

ALICE SPRINGS DESERT PARK

If you have always wanted to trek through Australia's fascinating desert landscape, then this one's for you. The huge area, a mixture of museum and zoological garden, gives a good idea of the natural history of the surrounding desert. One highlight is the Nocturnal House – home to a whole range of endangered desert dwellers.

INSIDER TIP
Night at the animal park

Night is definitely the liveliest time here, and you can experience it first hand on the Nocturnal Tour (A$45). *Daily 7.30am–6pm | A$32, children A$16 | Larapinta Drive | alicespringsdesertpark.com.au | ⊙ 2–3 hrs*

SHOPPING

Traditional art created in the desert community of Papunya, 240km northwest of Alice Springs, is not only a beautiful souvenir, but – depending on the artist – can also be an investment. Direct sales of works from Papunya can be found at *Papunya Tula Artists (63 Todd Mall | papunyatula. com.au).* Ask for a certificate of authenticity for more expensive works! For more information see: *ankaaa.org.au* and *desart.com.au.*

SPORT & ACTIVITIES

Digeridoo crash course, anyone? The *Sounds of Starlight Theatre* offers half-hour taster sessions for just A$10 *(Mon–Fri 11–11.30am | 40 Todd Mall | tel. 08 89 53 08 26 | soundsof starlight.com).*

NIGHTLIFE

The Rock Bar (78 Todd Street) is a good place for a drink, as is *Todd Tavern (1 Todd Mall).* But a word of warning: there have been repeated confrontations between drunken locals and tourists, especially at night.

AROUND ALICE SPRINGS

6 HERMANNSBURG

This village west of Alice Springs (pop. 600) has a former Lutheran *missionary station (daily 9am–5pm | A$12 | ⊙ 1 hr)* that was founded in 1877. The informative and moving exhibition is a reminder of controversial attempts by the church to convert Indigenous Australians to Christianity by trying to enforce values of "order and discipline".

Well-known former residents of Hermannsburg include the painter Albert Namatjira (1902–59), founder of a new, rather Western landscape painting style of the outback *(Hermannsburg School),* and ethnologist Ted Strehlow (1908–78), leading researcher of the culture of the Central Australian Arrarnta people. *hermannsburg.com.au | ▢ E4*

7 KINGS CANYON (WATARRKA)

470km / 6 hrs from Alice Springs by car
The steep gorge with its weathered

Art on display, and for sale, in the Papunya Tula Gallery in Alice Springs

peaks today attracts almost as many visitors as Uluru. But do not miss Kings Canyon. There are asphalted roads from Uluru via the *Lasseter Highway* and *Luritja Road* to this rocky landscape, which is millions of years old. Alternatively, take the route along *Larapinta Drive* via Hermannsburg, which should only be tackled in a 4 × 4. You need to be fairly fit for the three-to four-hour *Canyon Walk* around the gorge. It's best to start early in the morning – and be sure to take plenty of water with you! If that sounds a bit too much like hard work, the 45-minute *Kings Creek Walk* is easier and has more shade. *E4*

8 ULURU-KATA TJUTA NATIONAL PARK ★ 🛉

468km / 5 hrs 45 mins from Alice Springs by car

Uluru, or *Ayers Rock*, as it used to be called, can be reached from Alice Springs in a normal car along a tarmacked road.

There are also shuttle buses between Alice Springs and Ayers Rock Resort *(approx. 5½ hrs | A$125 one way | emurun.com.au)*.

This 348-m-high monolith which, rather like an iceberg, reaches miles down into the ground below it, attracts hundreds of thousands of visitors every year to the red heart of the continent. For Anangu people, however, it is the site with the greatest spiritual meaning and an important testimony to their Story of Creation. Since 1985, Uluru and "neighbouring" Kata Tjuta have been made into a national park covering 1325km² and have been returned to the Anangu.

The entrance to the park *(A$25/ person)* is about 15km from Uluru. There are two car parks along this stretch from where you can watch the sunrise or sunset. Please note: alcohol is forbidden (although organised tour groups are exempted). There are also several car parks at Uluru itself from which you can explore the base of the rock. The *Ayers*

Rock Resort (ayersrockresort.com.au) in *Yulara* is the supply centre for Uluru, approx. 15km from the rock and 6km from the airport. It has a pizzeria and snack bars, a supermarket, booking offices, souvenir and textiles shops, hotels of every category, and a campsite.

For decades, information boards placed on behalf of the Anangu asked tourists to refrain from climbing Uluru – unfortunately without much success. Since 2019, there has been an official ban on tourists climbing the mountain. In any case, it's more beautiful from below: the 9.4-km Base Walk takes you around the monolith in about three hours. The park rangers offer free guided walks every day *(Oct–April 8am, May–Sep 10am | from Mala Walk Car Park)*. You'll find many other tours and activities, some free of charge, at the *Tours & Information Centre (daily 8am–7pm)* of the Ayers Rock Resort (Yulara). On the *SEIT Uluru Tour (A$95)*, for instance, the mythology associated with the rock is explained, and visitors are shown how local Anangu people have survived in this apparently inhospitable land for thousands and thousands of years. At the *Uluru-Kata Tjuta Cultural Centre (daily 7am–6pm | admission free | short.travel/aus15)*, you will find out what other activities are available in the national park, you can visit an interesting exhibition on Anangu culture and see the nature in the park. It is the perfect starting point for a visit to Uluru.

The *Sounds of Silence Dinner (approx. A$200 per person | short. travel/aus14)* is unforgettable: You sit at beautifully laid tables some

distance from Uluru at sunset and enjoy a wonderful buffet meal. As it gets dark, a sparkling firmament unfolds above you.

INSIDER TIP
Dinner under the stars

About 50km from Uluru is *Kata Tjuta*, a collection of 36 rounded, domed rocks over an area of 35km². The highest of these "heads" (*Kata Tjuta* means "many heads") is almost 200m higher than Uluru, and many visitors much prefer the Olgas, as the rock formation used to be known, to the far more famous Uluru. Enjoy the rich orange hues of the Central Australian desert on a lovely walk through the mountains. A hike through the *Valley of the Winds* takes

You can't climb it, but a walk around the base of Uluru is well worth it

around three hours and is particularly recommended. But don't underestimate the weather: in the cooler months, icy winds howl through the gorges (be sure to take a coat and hat); in summer, the high temperatures turn the rocks into a gigantic oven, so it's best to set off early in the morning with plenty of water and an insect net for your head! *E4*

A GOOD NIGHT'S SLEEP

SNOOZE BY THE CANYON

A glass of wine in hand, a soft mattress to lie on and the rugged bushland all around. Granted, it's more glamping than camping here, 36km from Kings Canyon. *Kings Creek Station (tel. 08 89 56 74 74 | kingscreek station.com.au | $-$$)* offers three luxury tents and 25 cabins, as well as a more traditional tent area.

POOL PLUS BAR AT KAKADU

The point that some maps call Cooinda actually only refers to *Cooinda Lodge (tel. 08 89 79 15 00 | kakadutourism.com | $-$$$)*. You have the choice of 48 rooms and a lovely campsite, and everything is arranged around a central pool with a bar and restaurant.

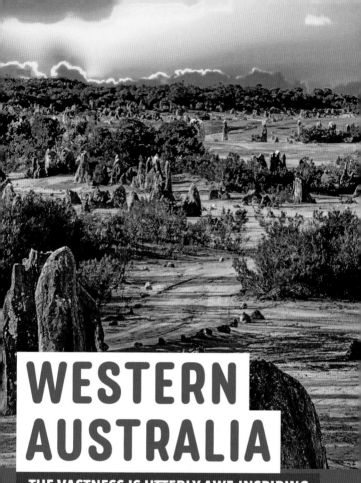

WESTERN AUSTRALIA

THE VASTNESS IS UTTERLY AWE-INSPIRING

Were you to divide the land area of Western Australia – WA for short – equally among its population, then every single individual, from the tiniest baby to the oldest senior citizen would have their very own square kilometre.

Slightly less than 2.6 million people live on the 2.5 million km² of this land mass, which is one-third of the entire continent. The region is as varied as it is vast, ranging from the fabulous surfing beaches

The Pinnacles create an other-worldly landscape in the desert

and idyllic wine-growing areas in the south, to bizarre landscapes such as the Pinnacles, Karjini National Park and Purnululu National Park, and isolated Ningaloo Reef and the Kimberleys in the north.

From cosmopolitan Perth, you can comfortably explore the south-west in a week or two. A trip to the vast, uninhabited north promises fabulous highlights, but allow at least four weeks for the route from Perth to Darwin.

WESTERN AUSTRALIA

INDIAN
OCEAN

Port Hedland

Karratha

1370km, 14 hrs

Exmouth p. 132

Cape Range National Park 11

Karijini National Park 12

Ningaloo Reef ★ 10

Coral Bay

Newma

Coral Bay

Carnarvon

1250km, 13 hrs

Monkey Mia 13

Denham

95

Meekat

Kalbarri

Geraldton

Mullewa

123

Mount Mag

95

Pinnacles (Nambung) National Park ★ 2

Southern C

Merredin

Joondalup

Perth ★ p. 126

Brookton

Rottnest Island 1

Mandurah

Kondinin

Wave Ro

3

Cottesloe Beach

Bunbury 9

Collie

Newdeg

Cape Naturaliste Lighthouse 7

Yallingup 6 8 Busselton

Katanning

Yallingup Beach

Margaret River p. 129

Manjimup

Cape Leeuwin 5

Mount Barker

Kimberley★
p. 137

✈

● **Kununurra**
p. 138

Cape Leveque **17**

☂
☀

Cable Beach

Derby **18**

1045km, 11 hrs

● Kalkarindji

19 Purnululu National Park

roome★
p. 134

14 Gantheaume Point
15 Malcolm Douglas Crocodile Park
16 Willie Creek Pearl Farm

○ Bililuna

○ Balgo

5

Nyirripi ○

AUSTRALIA

einster

○ Laverton

Leonora

✈
4 Kalgoorlie-Boulder

○ Kambalda

○ Norseman

1

○ Salmon Gums

✈
Esperance

MARCO POLO HIGHLIGHTS

★ **PERTH**
The world's most remote city – yet still confident, bright and futuristic ➤ p. 126

★ **PINNACLES (NAMBUNG) NATIONAL PARK**
Bizarre, towering rock needles in the middle of a lonely, sandy desert ➤ p. 128

★ **WAVE ROCK**
It's not just the sea that makes waves ➤ p. 128

★ **NINGALOO REEF**
One of the most beautiful and varied coral reefs in the world, home to so many sea creatures ➤ p. 132

★ **BROOME**
Dreamy beaches meet ancient rocks and dinosaur footprints ➤ p. 134

★ **KIMBERLEY**
Unique wilderness and terrain for adventure seekers ➤ p. 137

▲
N
250 km
155 mi

PERTH

(📖 B6) **Thanks to its modern skyline and a futuristic beach promenade, your first impression of ★ Perth (pop. 2.1 million) may well be that of a Gulf metropolis.**

In the past 20 years, a boom in raw materials has seen Perth grow rapidly, but Western Australia's capital remains what it has always been: an attractive and relaxed city that is a great place to live, with lots of sunshine and nature-loving locals who are only too happy to exchange shirt and tie for a Neoprene wetsuit and surfboard. You can get to 🏄 *Cottesloe Beach*, one of the loveliest city beaches, from the city centre in about 30 minutes by train and bus.

🚌 Four free bus routes serve Perth's centre *(Free Transit Zone | short.travel/ aus21)*: the red and yellow CAT buses run east to west; the blue run north to south and the green are in the west.

WHERE TO START?

Many sights can be reached on foot from the pedestrianised **City Mall** *(Murray Street/Hay Street)*, including the newly designed banks of the Swan River, with the sound of The Swan Bells, and the City Railway Station, where regional trains also stop, e.g. from Fremantle. The bus terminal is opposite the station. You can leave your car at your accommodation, as there are free buses in the city.

SIGHTSEEING

KINGS PARK

Just a few minutes from the city centre, the park is an oasis of peace for those who are tired from walking everywhere. Enjoy lovely panoramic views from *Kings Park Lookout* and *DNA Observation Tower. bgpa.wa.gov.au/ kings-park*

THE SWAN BELLS

If the sound of the bells in this bell tower *(Mon, Thu noon–1pm)* seems familiar, then that's because you've been to London. They were based on the bells of St Martin-in-the-Fields. *Daily 10am–4.30pm | A$18 | Barrack Square | thebelltower.com.au*

PERTH MINT

This is where you can see the world's largest collection of gold nuggets and watch while the precious metal is cast. *Daily 9am–5pm | A$19 | 310 Hay Street | perthmint.com.au. | ⏱ 1.5 hrs*

FREMANTLE

Beautiful, restored buildings give Perth's port a special charm of its very own. Good restaurants *(e.g. on Fishing Boat Harbour)* and cafés on South Street, shops and markets *(Fremantle Markets | Fri 8am–8pm, Sat & Sun 8am–6pm | Henderson Street/South Terrace | freemantlemarkets.com.au)* attract visitors – either by train or boat from Swan Bell Tower/Barrack Street Jetty in Perth. Another main attraction is *Fremantle Prison (daily 9am–5pm | tour A$22 | 1 The Terrace | fremantle prison.com.au | ⏱ 1–2 hrs).* For more

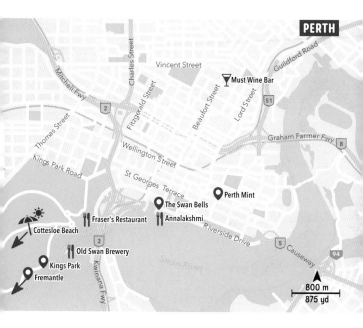

than 140 years, this prison kept Western Australia's most dangerous criminals from the outside world. *visit fremantle.com.au*

EATING & DRINKING

ANNALAKSHMI 🐷
This eatery right on the Swan River (behind the Bell Tower) offers a great Indian vegetarian buffet. Once you've polished off your meal, you get to decide for yourself how much to leave to cover the bill. *Daily | tel. 08 92 21 30 03 | annalakshmi.com.au*

FRASER'S RESTAURANT
It's hard to say which is better: the view or the food. The No. 1 address for special occasions (you're sure to think of one) offers fabulous views of Kings Park and the city. Try the melt-in-the-mouth fresh squid. *Daily | Fraser Av. | Kings Park | tel. 08 94 81 71 00 | frasersrestaurant.com. au | $$$*

INSIDER TIP
For seafood fans

OLD SWAN BREWERY
Brewery restaurant on the river with a surprisingly wide range of dishes and its own excellent home-brewed beer. *Daily | 173 Mounts Bay Road | Crawley | tel. 08 92 11 89 99 | theoldbrewery. com.au | $$*

SHOPPING

The *Forrest Chase (forrestchase.com. au)* shopping complex between Wellington, Murray and Barrack Street and Forrest Place offers endless opportunities to update your wardrobe.

NIGHTLIFE

Xpress (xpressmag.com.au) – Perth's free magazine that appears every Thursday – lists everything that is hip in the city right now and which live bands are appearing where. Nightlife is largely concentrated in *Subiaco (Hay Street)*.

MUST WINE BAR

The incredible wine list offers a choice of 40 different wines by the glass and 500 by the bottle. French snacks are also served. *Daily | 519 Beaufort Street | tel. 08 93 28 82 55 | must.com.au*

AROUND PERTH

■ ROTTNEST ISLAND

18km / 1 hr 30 mins from Perth by ferry

The 11-km-long and 5-km-wide island off Perth is a good weekend destination and home of the quokka, a marsupial that is only found here. The best way to get there is by ferry *(return ticket A$69 | rottnestexpress.com.au).* Cars aren't allowed on the island, but you can easily reach the beautiful beaches by bike. Information, including bike hire: *Rottnest Island Visitor Centre (tel. 08 94 32 93 00 | rottnest island.com) | ▥ B6*

■ PINNACLES (NAMBUNG) NATIONAL PARK ★

190km / 2 hrs 20 mins from Perth by car

A paradise for photographers. The spectacular collection of limestone pillars in the Nambung National Park is best visited early in the morning for perfect light conditions. Lot's wife could possibly have met her fate here (as described in the Bible) if the rocks were of salt, as at least some of the Pinnacles look like people turned to stone. If you take the 5-km circuit route through the forest of pillars or pose for a photo between the boulders, you really can believe such a story. It has been worked out that the Pinnacles – some up to 5m high – were created between 150,000 and 80,000 years ago. The sun baked hollow trunk-like formations in the desert: the granules of sand blown by the wind solidified into limestone columns on which more sand became stuck. ▥ A5

INSIDER TIP
Pillars at sunrise

■ WAVE ROCK ★

340km / 3 hrs 45 mins from Perth by car

Who says waves can only exist in water? Wave Rock is an imposing rock formation shaped like a 15-m-high wave, 340km southeast of Perth near the town of Hyden. This huge wave was created by the wind and weather: heat, frost and flood waters that, over the course of time, left their mark in the form of strange striped patterns. Wave Rock is more than two million years old. ▥ B6

4 KALGOORLIE BOULDER

600km / 6 hrs 30 mins from Perth by car

Granted, a trip from Perth to the goldfields in the east is more than a mere excursion. But if you happen to be on your way to South Australia or the Red Centre, why not stop to see the precious metal for yourself. Discovered in 1892, the gold reserves are still one of the main reasons for the affluence of Western Australia today. The area is characterised by open-cut mines. The best way to explore them is on a tour. For information: *Kalgoorlie-Boulder Tourist Centre (tel. 08 90 21 19 66 | kalgoorlie tourism.com)* | ⌂ C5

MARGARET RIVER

(⌂ B6) **Waves, wine and wellness: in only 50 years, the idyllic provincial town of Margaret River (pop. 6,300) close to the breathtaking coast, has become a first-class wine-growing region.**

Many of the 200 wineries offer wine-tasting and some also have excellent restaurants. Paths lead through secluded woods; you can find beaches with sensational surfing along the rocky coast between Cape Naturaliste and Cape Leeuwin, with more sheltered bathing spots around sandy Geographe Bay. Between June and December whales visit the coastal

The sculptural power of nature is on display at Wave Rock

Find your favourite tipple at one of the many wineries and breweries around Margaret River

waters and, with a bit of luck, you can sometimes see them from the shore.

EATING & DRINKING

COLONIAL BREWING CO
Why not take home one of the various types of home-brewed beer, including *Kolsch Ale*, that is very similar to the German beer of a similar name. It's available in bottles to take away or to be drunk in the pub or in its lovely beer garden – you could even stop for lunch. Live music Sunday lunchtimes. *Daily until 6pm, Fri until 10pm | Osmington Road | tel. 08 97 58 81 77 | colonialbrewingco.com.au | $–$$*

MARGARET RIVER CHOCOLATE COMPANY
A must for the sweet-toothed, but also a treat for fans of all things spicy. In this small factory, the delicious chocolate is sometimes mixed with spices such as chilli pepper. *415 Harman's Mill | chocolatefactory.com.au*

SHOPPING

ART
Many artists and craftspeople have settled in this attractive area. Most studios and galleries are between Margaret River and Yallingup or Dunsborough. A small selection of exquisite, high-quality objects is on sale in *Yallingup Galleries (Caves Road/Gunyulgup Valley Road)*, including works by the contemporary artist Judy Prosser, whose work incorporates Aboriginal motifs. For further addresses, see: *margaretriver artisans.com.au*.

WINE

The *Regional Wine Centre (9 Bussel Highway | mrwines.com)* provides a good overview of the location of local wineries and the wines they produce. A tasting session (and lunch) can be recommended at *Hamelin Bay Wines (199 McDonald Road | Karridale | approx. 32km to the south)*, with a beautiful view from the dining terrace. Also good is the stylish winery *Leeuwin Estate (Stevens Road | leeuwinestate.com.au)* which has an art gallery and an excellent restaurant *(daily at lunchtime, Sat also in the evening | tel 08 97 59 00 00 | $$$).*

AROUND MARGARET RIVER

5 CAPE LEEUWIN

51km / 40 mins from Margaret River by car

Bussel Highway leads to the infamous rocky headland in the south feared by seafarers and battered by breakers. Beyond Augusta, the last settlement of any size, the tall slim *lighthouse (daily 9am–5pm | A$8, guided tour A$20 | booking tel. 08 97 57 74 11 | short.travel/aus46 | ⏱ 1 hr)* comes into sight. A guided tour will take you up to the all-round lookout with breathtaking distant views. 📖 B6

6 YALLINGUP

42km / 40 mins from Margaret River by car

Finally: the perfect wave. Yallingup's 🏄 beaches are the stuff of legend in surfing circles. Don't worry, you don't have to be a pro surfer to make the most of this pretty coastal village. The beaches were practically made for dreamy walks; keep your eyes peeled – dolphins often frolic in the waves here. 📖 B6

7 CAPE NATURALISTE LIGHTHOUSE

60km / 50 mins from Margaret River by car

The massive lighthouse and the *maritime museum* document the adventurous seafaring history here in Geographe Bay. A guided tour also includes the platform around the lantern room where you gaze far out into the Indian Ocean. Whales can be seen between September and December. *Daily 9am–5pm | A$5 | short.travel/aus47 | ⏱ 1 hr | 📖 B6*

8 BUSSELTON

40km / 40 mins from Margaret River by car

White sandy beaches have made this coastal town (pop. 37,000) a popular place for a summer break. There are enough good places to stay here at *Geographe Bay* for a few relaxing days. The pier that extends 1.8km into the water is the longest in the Southern Hemisphere. A small railway along its length takes you to the *Underwater Observatory (daily guided tours on the hour 9am–5pm | A$34 incl. train ride |*

busseltonjetty.com.au | ⏲ 2 hrs) where you can get up close to the sea life. 🕮 *B6*

9 BUNBURY

100km / 1 hr 15 mins from Margaret River by car

The old harbour town of Bunbury (pop. 33,000) is becoming more and more popular as a holiday resort, due in no small part to the tame dolphins that regularly visit the bay. At the *Dolphin Discovery Centre (Dec–April, daily 8am–4pm, boat tours all year round | Koombana Drive | tel. 08 97 91 30 88 | dolphindiscovery.com.au ⏲ 1.5 hrs)*, you can observe these marine mammals from a boat *(A$54)* or up close in the water *(A$165, book in advance!). visitbunbury.com.au | 🕮 B6*

LIMESTONE CAVES

There are about 330 caves in the karst landscape around Margaret River. The few that are open to the public are on Caves Road. Before you disappear underground, visit the *Lake Cave Interpretive Centre (daily 9am–5pm | admission free | ⏲ 30 mins)*, 18km north of Margaret River, where films and animations provide comprehensive information on the caves and their fragile ecosystem. The main subterranean attraction is the *Jewel Cave (daily tours 9.30am–3.30pm every hour | A$23 | 35km south | short. travel/aus22 | ⏲ 1 hr)*, simply on account of its glittering illuminations that are turned on at the flick of a switch. Guided tours are more adventurous through the more natural world of stalactites and stalagmites in

Ngilgi Cave (daily 9.30am–4pm | from A$23 | Yallingup | 40km north of Yallingup | short.travel/aus23 | ⏲ 1 hr). 🕮 *B6*

EXMOUTH

(🕮 *A4*) **The small town of Exmouth (pop. 2,200) at the tip of North West Cape has evolved into a starting point for tourists who want to explore one of the last virtually untouched coral reefs in the world.**

The Ningaloo Reef is a prize jewel in Australia's natural treasure trove. The national park itself is largely untouched, but you'll still find all the usual home comforts in Exmouth, especially at the modern *marina* which has posh hotels and good restaurants.

AROUND EXMOUTH

10 NINGALOO REEF ★

150km / 1 hr 40 mins from Exmouth by car

Ningaloo Reef is widely regarded as one of the best places in the world to dive or snorkel. The 260-km-long reef, a Unesco World Heritage Site since 2011, stretches from the small coastal village of *✱ Coral Bay (coralbay.org)* along the peninsula to the north. Its beauty and variety are absolutely on a par with the Barrier Reef to the east of

Snorkel with giant but harmless whale sharks on Ningaloo Reef

Australia. Ningaloo Reef is home to at least 250 different types of coral and 500 species of fish. The confluence of ocean currents rich in nutrients and its proximity to the Continental Shelf, explain why there are so many different species. Four species of ocean turtle live on the reef, as do manta rays, humpback whales, dugongs and various kinds of shark. Ningaloo Reef has gained a reputation as being one of the very few places where whale sharks can be watched from close quarters. You can swim with these marine animals that grow to up to 18m long – and "no worries": these huge beasts are plankton eaters and are not dangerous at all.

Ningaloo Reef can be reached on foot from the mainland. In lagoons such as *Turquoise Bay*, 60km south of Exmouth, you can take a look at the variety of coral and fish in waist-deep water equipped with just goggles and a snorkel. Diving tours are organised by tour operators, e.g. *Ningaloo Reef Dive (from A$130 | ningalooreefdive. com)*, to the outer reaches and snorkelling expeditions visit the whale sharks. High season is between April and June. ⌂ A4

🔟 CAPE RANGE NATIONAL PARK

35km / 45 mins from Exmouth by car

The national park bordering Ningaloo Reef is outstanding due to its number of unique geological features, fossils and its 630 flowering plant species. *Ningaloo Safari Tours (A$240 | 23 Ningaloo Street | Exmouth | tel. 08 99 49 15 50 | ningaloosafari.com)* will show you the park's beauty complete with campground and great camping spots. ⌂ A4

12 KARIJINI NATIONAL PARK

640km / 8 hrs from Exmouth by car
Karijini is the second largest national park in the state, covering 6,000km² and, with its orangey-red rock formations, its scenery is considered the most spectacular. Accommodation and provisions are available in *Tom Price* and *Paraburdoo*. Camping is permitted in the park. *short.travel/aus48* | ☐ B4

13 MONKEY MIA

705km / 7 hrs 30 mins from Exmouth by car
In Monkey Mia, halfway between Perth and Exmouth, you can watch dolphins at close quarters. Most mornings the animals swim right next to the beach of the *Monkey Mia Reserve (A$10, families A$28 | monkeymia dolphins.org)* and can be fed – strictly regulated – standing knee-deep in the water. Tens of thousands of visitors come to this area of Shark Bay every year, although whether or not it's to feed the dolphins is a matter of some dispute. Critics believe that feeding makes the animals dependent on humans.

INSIDER TIP
The cradle of life

The *Hamelin Pool Marine Nature Reserve (short.travel/aus51)* offers a unique chance to meet the oldest lifeform on our planet: the stromalites. These fossils, created by microorganisms and scattered here in the warm ocean, are already a whopping 3.5 billion years old. ☐ A4

BROOME

(☐ C2) **Sailing yachts glide across the velvety water, and there's camel trekking on the beach. And when the glowing red tropical sun sinks beyond the horizon in Kimberley's secret capital of ★ Broome (pop. 14,000), the town briefly holds it breath.**

This natural spectacle, which happens every evening and which attracts both residents and tourists who wait for it with folding chairs and cans of beer, is just one of the reasons why Broome is becoming more and more popular as a travel destination – it is also becoming the chosen home for Australians wishing to escape the winter. In its favour are the pleasant climate and the relaxed, tropical lifestyle of the "pearling town". Until 1920, Broome was the world's leading centre for pearl farming and the production of mother-of-pearl. And although tourism has largely replaced pearl farming as the main industry, those who wish to buy pearls here will still have plenty of choice.

EATING & DRINKING

BAY CLUB

You have to ask yourself what's better: the fabulous views over Roebuck Bay, or the mouth-watering sight of the catch of the day on your plate. The grilled specialities are especially popular. *Daily | 47 Carnavon Street | in the Mangrove Resort | tel. 08 91 92 13 03 | mangrovehotel.com.au | $$–$$$*

There's an abundance of pearls in Broome

MATSO'S BREWERY

A legend in Broome. Home-brewed beer, burgers and the best company. *Daily | 60 Hammersly Street | tel. 08 91 93 58 11 | matsos.com.au | $$*

SHOPPING

You can purchase pearls from *Willie Creek Pearl Farm* in the centre *(32 Blackman Street)* and on Cable Beach *(2 Challenor Drive)*.

BEACHES

CABLE BEACH

This fine sandy beach is 22km long – no wonder it is the town's main attraction. Part of the fun is enjoying a leisurely beach ride on a camel – so make sure to jump into the saddle with *Broome Camel Safaris (from A$35 | broomecamelsafaris.com.au)*,

for example. The phenomenon called the *Staircase to the Moon* that can be seen here is a unique natural spectacle. The unforgettable sight occurs between March and October on three days every month, when the full moon is reflected in the grooves left in the sand by the receding tide. Exact dates can be obtained at *short.travel/aus52*.

INSIDER TIP
Staircase to the moon

AROUND BROOME

14 GANTHEAUME POINT

8km / 12 mins from Broome by car
Can rocks really be this red? At the south-western tip of Broome in front

of the turquoise sea, sandstone boulders are stacked in curious piles – a sight well worth the short hike (about 200m from the car park). At extremely low tide, the waves recede to reveal 130-million-year-old dinosaur footprints. Note: the last 2km to the car park are dirt roads and may be impassable during the rainy season. 📖 C2

🖾 MALCOLM DOUGLAS CROCODILE PARK 👪

16km / 15 mins from Broome by car
Wildlife film-maker Malcolm Douglas, the real "Crocodile Dundee", made a name for himself catching dangerous saltwater crocodiles. He was killed in a car accident in 2010, but his legacy lives on. In his large park, more than 200 crocodiles and other wild animals can be seen. *Daily 2–5pm, crocodile feeding 3pm | A\$35, children A\$20, families A\$90 | Great Northern Highway | malcolmdouglas.com.au | ⏱ 2 hrs | 📖 C2*

🖾 WILLIE CREEK PEARL FARM

40km / 50 mins from Broome by car
This pearl farm offers a good introduction into the art of pearl farming. *A\$75, 5-hr bus tour from Broome A\$120 | tour reservation tel. 08 91 92 00 00 | williecreekpearls.com.au | ⏱ 1.5 hrs | 📖 C2*

🖾 CAPE LEVEQUE

208km / 4 hrs from Broome by car
If you're in the mood for an all-terrain adventure, then the Dampier Peninsula is just the place for you. Local Aboriginal peoples have been granted native title rights to much of this area. A sand and dust track leads to Cape Leveque, where you can fish or

Leave footsteps in the sand on the isolated beaches around Cape Leveque

sunbathe on deserted beaches. Accommodation is few and far between, so be sure to book in advance – even the campsite! ⟐ C2

18 DERBY

220km / 2 hrs 30 mins from Broome by car

Admittedly, this small town (pop. 3,300) on the edge of the Kimberley region is not all that much to look at and historically it is known for all the wrong reasons too: during World War II, a few Japanese bombs fell in Derby, and in more recent years illegal immigrants have been detained here. But you don't come to Derby for the town, you come for the sensational *Horizontal Waterfalls* in Talbot Bay – a bay where the strong current sends water shooting through the narrow island crevices. There are flights from

Broome as well as day tours with, for example, *Go Horizontal Falls Tour (A$800 | gohorizontalfallstours.com.au).* ⟐ C2

KIMBERLEY

(⟐ C–D2) **Only the most adventurous visitors make it to the vast ★ Kimberley region in the north. Massive canyons, waterfalls, endless horizons and unique rock paintings attract people to the far north of Western Australia.**

Huge swathes of this nature reserve, which covers 424,000km² between the towns of Broome in the west and Kununurra in the east, are almost entirely uninhabited. The largely untouched scenery is some of the most beautiful Australia has to offer. A journey through Kimberley not only is time-consuming, but it can also be a real challenge. It's vital you take the time to plan well. For detailed information see *kimberleyaustralia.com*.

Although the Great Northern Highway, that runs 1,000km from Broome to Kununurra, is passable all year round, detours to the countless canyons can only be made in a 4×4. During the wet season, from November to April, large areas are completely submerged. The best time to travel is May/June and September/October. In July and August many motels and campsites, even in the most remote areas, are fully booked.

The Gibb River Road is only passable in the dry season and in an all-terrain vehicle

SIGHTSEEING

GIBB RIVER ROAD

This unsurfaced road leads to the best-known gorges in Devonian Reef, the main attractions in the Kimberley region. They are, however, only passable by motor vehicle in the dry season, i.e. not between December and April, and the Gibb River Road should only be tackled in a 4×4. Inform yourself beforehand about its condition at the *Main Road Department (tel. 08 91 68 47 77 | mainroads.wa.gov.au | short.travel/aus45).*

KUNUNURRA

(*□ D2*) **This small town (pop. 5,300) on the border with the Northern Territory was only built in the 1960s, during the construction of the massive Ord River dam.**

Boat trips are offered on *Lake Argyle*, the reservoir that was created covering more than 1,000km². Venture out to *El Questro Wilderness Park (May–Oct | elquestro.com.au)*, which has a variety of different types of accommodation. Kununurra is the ideal starting point for tours and spectacular scenery is guaranteed.

AROUND KUNUNURRA

🔟 PURNULULU NATIONAL PARK

291km / 4 hrs 15 mins from Kununurra by car

A visit to this national park is only possible in the dry season, from around May to September. The lichen-streaked *Bungle Bungle Range* sandstone formations in various shades are 300km south of Kununurra and are just as spectacular as Uluru (Ayers Rock). From the Great Northern Highway, the park can only be reached by 4×4s, even in good weather as the dirt track crosses several watercourses. *hallscreektourism.com.au* | 🗺 *D2*

A GOOD NIGHT'S SLEEP

(NOT) JUST FOR BIRDWATCHERS

The beautiful *BBO Campground (Crab Creek Road | 6km unsurfaced road | tel. 08 91 93 56 00 | broome birdobservatory.com | $)* is on Roebuck Bay, approx. 25km from Broome. The campsite might not have electricity, but it does come with some pretty special views: this bird observatory is considered by ornithologists to be one of the five most important in the world.

HIDDEN LUXURY

The *Hidden Valley Forest Retreat (Hagg Road | approx. 30km north of Margaret River | tel. 08 97 55 10 66 | yourhiddenvalley.com | $$$)*, with four secluded eco-chalets scattered around the bushland, guarantees absolute privacy. And if you don't feel like cooking dinner yourself, the chef will come and conjure up a private gourmet meal.

SOUTH AUSTRALIA

DESERT, WINE & BROAD HORIZONS

Red sand, green vineyards, strange rock formations and no end of wildlife: South Australia means undiluted adventure in the outback.

Around 1.8 million people live in this state which covers just under one million km². Most live in the attractive and cultivated capital, Adelaide, and in the fertile plains around South Australia's life giving artery, the huge Murray River. In the agricultural areas in the south, vines, fruit and cereals are grown. In the west and north these

Shiraz grapes thrive in the warm and dry conditions of Mclaren Vale

soon give way to extensive cattle- and sheep-farming regions, and then into arid zones and fascinating desert. Dotted all over the place are hidden oases, which have a great variety of plants and animals.

After rare but often heavy rainfall, everything bursts into life, even in the driest of areas. Carpets of wild flowers shoot up, insects buzz about, birds collect around the suddenly created lakes and ponds, and kangaroos and their smaller marsupial friends abound.

SOUTH AUSTRALIA

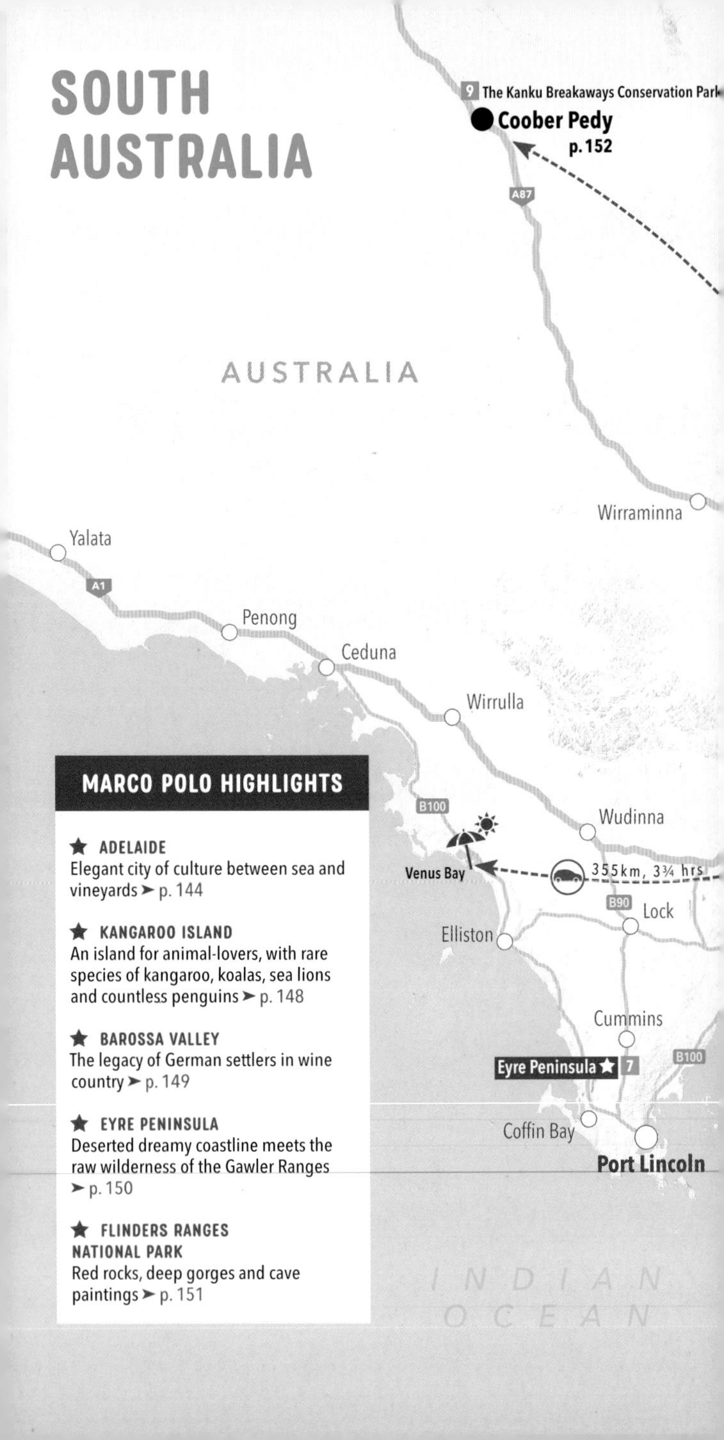

AUSTRALIA

9 The Kanku Breakaways Conservation Park
● **Coober Pedy**
p. 152

A87

Yalata

A1

Penong

Ceduna

Wirraminna

Wirrulla

B100

Wudinna

☀
☂
Venus Bay ←········🚗········ 355 km, 3¾ hrs

B90
Lock

Elliston

Cummins

Eyre Peninsula ★ 7
B100

Coffin Bay

Port Lincoln

I N D I A N
O C E A N

MARCO POLO HIGHLIGHTS

★ **ADELAIDE**
Elegant city of culture between sea and vineyards ➤ p. 144

★ **KANGAROO ISLAND**
An island for animal-lovers, with rare species of kangaroo, koalas, sea lions and countless penguins ➤ p. 148

★ **BAROSSA VALLEY**
The legacy of German settlers in wine country ➤ p. 149

★ **EYRE PENINSULA**
Deserted dreamy coastline meets the raw wilderness of the Gawler Ranges ➤ p. 150

★ **FLINDERS RANGES NATIONAL PARK**
Red rocks, deep gorges and cave paintings ➤ p. 151

Leigh Creek

540 km, 5½ hrs

A87

8 Flinders Ranges National Park ★

Hawker

Broken Hill

A32

B79

6 Port Augusta

420 km, 4¾ hrs

Orroroo

A1

Whyalla

A32

Burra

A1

Clare

5 Clare Valley

B64

Morgan

Wallaroo

Eudunda

A20

Loxton

Minlaton

4 Barossa Valley ★

Gawler

A20

A20

Henley Beach

Adelaide ★ p. 144

120 km, 30 mins

Port Noarlunga

3 Adelaide Hills

B57

Fleurieu Peninsula

1

Murray Bridge

B12

Kingscote

A8

Lameroo

2 Kangaroo Island ★

Victor Harbor

B1

B57

Tintinara

Seal Bay

100 km
62.13 mi

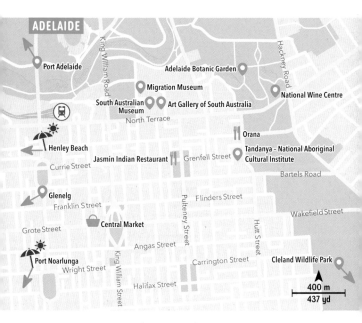

ADELAIDE

(⊞ F6) **Year after year, ★ Adelaide (pop. 1.3 million) safely secures a spot in the list of the world's top ten most liveable cities.**

WHERE TO START?

Victoria Square is a good starting point if you fancy something to eat in a Grote Street restaurant or want to take the tram to Glenelg. It's a 10-minute walk to **North Terrace**, the first address for the city's main attractions. And if you arrive by train, the railway station is also on North Terrace.

The city's tranquil charm is not always immediately apparent to visitors. Venture out to coastal suburbs like Brighton, Glenelg or Henley Beach, or take a trip to the Adelaide Hills and the wine regions of Barossa Valley and McLaren Vale. There's no doubt about it: life here is pretty sweet.

Just so you know, no convicts came to South Australia – a fact South Australians are keen to point out. Many of the European settlers who arrived in the first half of the 19th century were people who had to leave their native countries for religious or political reasons. Adelaide is still a tolerant, multicultural and cultivated city with numerous museums, theatres and concert halls.

The 🐷 *Adelaide Greeters (tel. 08 82 03 72 03 | short.travel/aus25)* will

---

be delighted to guide you around the city free of charge. Not only is this a great way to glean some background info, you might even make a new friend. Make sure to book at least three days in advance!

SIGHTSEEING

ART GALLERY OF SOUTH AUSTRALIA 🐖
A must for art lovers: with 35,000 works of art, the museum houses the second-biggest art collection in Australia. The Australian collection is particularly impressive. *Daily 10am-5pm | admission free | North Terrace | artgallery.sa.gov.au | ⊙ 1-2 hrs*

SOUTH AUSTRALIAN MUSEUM 👥 🐖
The longest snake – the wonambi – measures 6m from tip to tail, and crushes its prey to death. Thankfully, it has been extinct for around 40,000 years. You'll only encounter this devious representative of Australia's megafauna here at the museum – or rather, the fossil of one. Be sure to visit the Australian Aboriginal cultures gallery too. *Daily 10am-5pm | free guided tours 11am | admission free | North Terrace | samuseum.sa.gov.au | ⊙ 1.5 hrs*

MIGRATION MUSEUM
Did you know that German immigrants were instrumental in shaping Adelaide? Step into their shoes for an hour or two at the museum. *Daily 10am-5pm | admission free (donations welcome) | 82 Kintore Av. | migration.history.sa.gov.au | ⊙ 1.5 hrs*

TANDANYA – NATIONAL ABORIGINAL CULTURAL INSTITUTE 🐖
The cultural institute of the Kuarna people has art and craft galleries and changing exhibitions. There are often good *cultural performances* during the school holidays; information online. *Mon-Sat 10am-5pm | admission free | 253 Grenfell Street | tel. 08 82 24 32 00 | tandanya.com.au | ⊙ 1 hr*

ADELAIDE BOTANIC GARDEN 🐖
You might have spotted the large, eye-catching glass building when you approached Adelaide on the flight in. The greenhouse with brightly coloured birds and insects is only one of the highlights in this peaceful park. *Mon-Fri 7.15am-sunset, Sat, Sun from 9am, free guided tours daily 10.30am from Schomburgk Pavilion | admission free | North Terrace | short.travel/aus24 | ⊙ 1-2 hrs*

NATIONAL WINE CENTRE
The futuristic Wine Centre building is on the edge of the Botanic Garden. Interactive displays tell you everything you want to know about the wines of South Australia that is especially well known for its earthy, spicy reds. The centre has an excellent cellar where rare Australian wines can also be bought. *Wine tasting Mon-Wed 8am-6pm, Fri, Thu 8am-9pm, Sat 9am-9pm, Sun 9am-6pm | Yarrabee House | Botanic Road/Hackney Road | wineaustralia.com.au | ⊙ 1-2 hrs*

GLENELG 👯

The tram from Victoria Square to the most popular beach suburb in Adelaide takes about 20 minutes. Browse the shops on Jetty Road, grab a whoppingly big ice cream and stroll out onto the jetty. Catamarans run by *Temptation Sailing* leave from Holdfast Marina, just five minutes from the tram stop, for tours lasting three hours 30 minutes where you can swim with the dolphins *(from A$100, watching from A$70 | tel. 04 12 81 18 38 | dolphinboat.com.au)*.

INSIDER TIP
Swim with dolphins

PORT ADELAIDE

The historical port district in the north-west of the city keeps the city's early beginnings alive. The brochure "Walk the Port" from the visitor centre is a useful guide for a walk through the restored streets as well as for the lighthouse, erected in 1868, or the *South Australia Maritime Museum (Daily 10am–5pm | A$15, cheaper online | 126 Lipson Street | maritime.history. sa.gov.au | ⏱ 1.5 hrs)*, which is well worth visiting.

CLELAND WILDLIFE PARK 👯

Feed kangaroos and emus against the backdrop of the Adelaide skyline. This large park is the perfect chance to get up close and personal with the locals of the non-human variety. Animal feed is sold at the entrance. *Daily 9.30am–5pm | A$30, children A$15, families A$74 | 365 Mount Lofty Summit Road | Crafters | cleland wildlifepark.sa.gov.au | ⏱ 1.5 hrs*

The *Central Market* and neighbouring *Gouger Street* have the biggest selection of restaurants and cafés.

JASMIN INDIAN RESTAURANT

The scent of cumin, cardamom and nutmeg alone will make your mouth water. *Tue–Sat evening, also lunch on Thu & Fri | 31 Hindmarsh Square | tel. 08 82 23 78 37 | jasmin.com.au | $$*

ORANA

Acacia seeds and Australian mollusc: try something new in this restaurant, which is inspired by local Aboriginal cuisine. The seven- to nine-course tasting menu *(A$120)*, served on Friday lunchtimes only, is your chance to give it all a go. *Tue–Sat evenings only, Fri also at lunchtime | 285 Rundle Street | 1st floor | tel. 08 82 32 34 44 | restaurantorana.com | $$$*

INSIDER TIP
Tasting menu

Adelaide is good for opals, outback clothing, craft items and local art. *Rundle Mall* is the main shopping centre with shops, cafés and arcades and the often-photographed bronze pigs, as are King William Road (Hyde Park) and the *Jam Factory Contemporary Craft & Design (19 Morphett Street | jamfactory.com.au)*.

CENTRAL MARKET

The covered market has more than 80 stands with vegetables, fruit, fish and meat from the area. Asian and European dishes can be sampled at small stands. *Tue–Sat | Grote Street | adelaidecentralmarket.com.au*

BEACHES

Beautiful sandy beaches stretch along the entire coastline. The first ports of call from the city are *Glenelg* and *Henley Beach*. Carry on south for other great beaches popular with surfers: check out *Brighton*, *Port Noarlunga* and *Moana* beaches.

NIGHTLIFE

The Thursday supplement in the *Adelaide Advertiser* gives a what's on summary of theatre, concerts and exhibitions. Tickets for many events can be booked through *BASS (tel. 131 246 – ticket enquiries | bass.net.au).*

The premier live music venues for rock music are *Fowlers Live (68 North Terrace | fowlerslive.com.au)* and *Enigma Bar (173 Hindley Street | enigmabar.com.au).* Cultural events can also be found under *whatsonin adelaide.net.au*.

AROUND ADELAIDE

🚩 FLEURIEU PENINSULA
50km / 1 hr from Adelaide by car

For the people of Adelaide the peninsula located to the south is an attractive recreational area with sheltered beaches especially on the northwest coast. Inland, around rural *McLaren Vale*, there are more than a hundred wineries in this renowned

Adelaide Arcade is part of the Rundle Mall

wine-growing region. The local visitor centre *(Main Road | tel. 08 83 23 99 44 | mclarenvale.info)* can point those interested in wine-tasting in the right direction.

Goolwa on *Lake Alexandrina* is popular. It has a lovely beach, lots of restaurants and places to stay and the possibility to explore the *Coorong National Park* on a boat trip; *Coorong Cruises (from A$115 | tel. 08 85 55 22 03 | coorongcruises.com. au).* In cosy *Victor Harbor (holidayat victorharbor.com.au)* (pop. 15,000), pop into the *South Australian Whale Centre (daily 9am–5pm | A$9 | 2 Railway Terrace | sawhalecentre.com. au | ⏱ 1.5 hrs).* It provides information on the southern right whales, which can be seen here between June and September. *Granite Island* off Victor Harbor is home to around 2,000 tiny fairy penguins and can be reached across a wooden bridge on foot or on the historical horse-drawn tram *(daily 10am–4pm | return ticket A$10 | horsedrawntram.com.au).* ⊞ F6.

② KANGAROO ISLAND ★

120km / 30 mins from Adelaide by plane

Kangaroo Island is a paradise for animal- and nature-lovers. You can fly to the island from Adelaide in about 30 minutes, e.g. with *Regional Express/ Rex (rex.com.au)* or take the *Kangaroo Island Sealink Ferry (car and 2 people approx. A$400 | tel. 013 13 01 | sealink.com.au)* for the hour's crossing from Cape Jervis on the Fleurieu Peninsula to Penneshaw. Alternatively, there's passenger ferry company *kic*

(tel. 0419 10 01 00 | kic.com.au), which will take you to Kangaroo Island for just A$39 (one way). Once there,

they can help with car hire (from A$95/ day), as there is no public transport on the island.

More than half of Kangaroo Island is densely forested and more than 30 % of the bushland is a national park. Huge colonies of seals and sea lions occupy the island's beaches. Accompanied by rangers, a colony of several hundred sea lions can be visited in *Seal Bay Conservation Park (guided tours daily from 9am | from A$35)* on 🐾 *Seal Bay* in the south. In the evenings, pelicans crowd around the pier in *Kingscote*. In the winter, southern right whales rest out at sea. Those who don't just want to hike or animal-watch, can swim, surf, dive ride and cycle on Kangaroo Island, stock up on honey and eucalyptus oil prod-ucts – and eat very well too. Call in at

Island Beehive (59 Playford Hwy, Kingscote) and sample their exquisite Stringy Bark honey to really excite your tastebuds.

Day trips from Adelaide by bus and ferry last approx. 16 hours. But it's best to allow at least two days for the island. Good nature and self-drive tours are available through *Kangaroo Islands Odysseys (from A$460 | tel. 08 85 53 03 86 | kangarooislandodysseys. com.au).* Comprehensive information: tourkangarooisland.com.au. ⊞ F6–7

The vines in the Barossa Valley have German roots

⑶ ADELAIDE HILLS

27km / 35 mins from Adelaide by car

The gently rolling landscape of the Adelaide Hills starts some 27km from Adelaide. Fifty Lutheran migrant families who arrived in South Australia aboard the ship *Zebra*, founded the village of *Hahndorf* (pop. 2,700) in 1839. Half-timbered, German-style houses, an old German butcher's, a German inn, and antique clock museum and numerous souvenir shops and restaurants attract lots of tourists to Hahndorf every year. *adelaidehills.org.au* | ▥ *F6*

⑷ BAROSSA VALLEY ★

73km / 1 hr from Adelaide by car

Excellent wines, rye bread, sourdough, cheese, olives, smoked sausages and ham – and historical villages in pretty countryside: that's "The Barossa", north-east of Adelaide and a must for wine-lovers because it has more than 50 wineries. The first British farmers settled here in 1840. They were joined in 1842 by Lutherans from Silesia, Brandenburg and Poznan, who brought the first vines to the now world-famous wine-growing area.

The first German settlement,

Bethany, is a traditional elongated village with houses on one side of the road and small fields on the other. *Tanunda* (pop. 4,600), formerly Langmeil, is a good starting point for a ⚑ wine and gourmet tour through the region. It's a good idea to stay at least one night here in one of the many beautiful B&Bs offering vineyard views and sumptuous breakfasts. Pick up the *Winery Map* with a description of the *Scenic Drive 4* through the Barossa Valley at the *Barossa Wine & Visitor Centre (66–68 Murray Street | Tanunda | tel. 1300 85 29 82 | barossa. com)*. It is well worth stopping at the wineries on Para Road as well as at Penfolds, Charles Melton, Bethany Wines and Villa Tinto. The vast *Seppeltsfield Winery* has created its very own "archive": since 1878, a barrel of every vintage has been stored there in perpetuity. *⎯ F6*

🟥 CLARE VALLEY

140km / 2 hrs from Adelaide by car
North of Adelaide lies another idyllic wine-growing region. It's worth spending two days there, especially if you want to visit one or two of the prize-winning wineries. *Knappstein Wines (Mon–Fri 9am–5pm, Sat 11am–5pm, Sun 11am–4pm | 2 Pioneer Av. | tel. 08 88 41 21 00 | knappstein.com.au)* sets the standard for the very best-quality wines, both red and white. At *Skillogalee Wines (daily 8am–5pm | tel. 08 88 43 43 11 | skillogalee.com.au)*, you don't just get a light Riesling to drink but delicious lunches are also served. Those with at least one more day to spare

can explore the wine-growing area between *Auburn* and *Clare* by bike along the *Riesling Trail*. Bikes can be hired from *Clare Valley Cycle Hire (32 Victoria Road | 0418 80 20 77 | clare-valleycyclehire.com.au)*, while maps and further information are available from the *Clare Valley Wine, Food & Tourism Centre (8 Spring Gully Road | tel. 08 88 42 21 31 | clarevalley.com. au)*. *⎯ F6*

INSIDER TIP
Wine on two wheels

🟥 PORT AUGUSTA

305km / 3 hrs 30 mins from Adelaide by car
The harbour town (pop. 14,000) with a historic centre that is well worth visiting, is primarily a supply centre for the distant heartland further north, and is a *gateway to the outback*, both by road and rail: the Stuart Highway and legendary "Ghan" go from here to Darwin, and the Eyre Highway ends in Western Australia. An excellent insight into the outback and its extensive history is available at the *Wadlata Outback Centre (Mon–Fri 9am–5pm, Sat, Sun 10am–4pm | A$22 | 41 Flinders Terrace | wadlata.sa.gov. au | ⏱ 1.5 hrs)*. *⎯ F6*

🟥 EYRE PENINSULA ⭐

638km / 7 hrs from Adelaide by car
Wonderful coastline with fine sandy beaches are the trademark of this peninsula west of Adelaide. The desert plains and outback of the Gawler Ranges and the dried-up salt lake *Lake Gairdner* can be found further inland. Kangaluna Camp, a comfortable

campsite, is at the centre. From here it is around a two-hour drive to *Baird Bay*. This beautiful bay

is the perfect spot to swim with the sea lions and dolphins *(daily from 9am | A$180 | bairdbay.com)*, and these curious sea creatures are usually happy to get nose to nose. Why not make a detour to the gorgeous beach at 🌴 Venus Bay? 🗺 *E–F6*

8 FLINDERS RANGES NATIONAL PARK ★

420km / 4 hrs 45 mins from Adelaide by car

The bizarre rock formations that shimmer in reds and violets above the expanse of the plain more than 400km north of Adelaide make up this national park that covers 950km². Deep gorges cut through this largely arid region. Most tours and places to stay in this fantastic wilderness have to be booked beforehand in Adelaide. A 4×4 is only needed if you intend to leave the main route. *Wilpena Pound*, a huge area surrounded by jagged rocks, is the most characteristic landmark of the Flinders Ranges. Over 500 million years ago, this high plateau was at the bottom of the sea, as is confirmed by the countless fossils in the rocks. For accommodation, the *Wilpena Pound Resort (wilpenapound. com.au)* is a good choice and provides maps and information.

Iga Warta (tel. 08 86 48 37 37 | igawarta.com) is a cultural centre that introduces visitors to the culture of the Adnyamathanha people. Owner Cliff Coulthard, who helped in the safeguarding and interpretation of the cave paintings in Lascaux, France, shows his guests some of the many

Cliff Coulthard interprets the rock paintings in the Flinders Ranges

Life in a *dugout* in Coober Pedy

rock paintings and engravings in the gorges of the Flinders Ranges. Guests help hunt and collect bush food, hike or ride out on the family's horses into the heart of the mountains. Tours *(from A$75)* can last from just a few hours to several days. If you want to stay: pitch your tent on Iga Warta (near Copley), or stay in one of the rustic cabins or safari tents. *F5–6*

COOBER PEDY

(E5) **Raging heat by day, frost at night. And flies! The climate at Coober Pedy (pop. 3,500), halfway between Adelaide and Alice Springs, is so difficult that the whole town virtually lives underground. So why on earth would anyone even want to make this their home?**

Simple: around three-quarters of the world's white opals are found in and around Coober Pedy (from the Kokatha term *kuba piti* for "white man in a hole"). With daytime temperatures of up to 45°C and icy cold at night, it's not surprising that most people live in disused mines. Entire homes and even churches and hotels have been bored into the hillsides. The temperatures in the *dugouts* are a pleasant 24°C all year round.

A good insight into life here and the nature of the outback is provided on the *Mail Run (Mon & Thu 9am | 600km in about 12 hrs | approx.*

A$270 | tel. 08 86 72 52 26 | mailrun tour.com.au), which goes from Coober Pedy to *Oodnadatta* and *William Creek.* The destination of an hour-long sightseeing flight is *Anna Creek Painted Hills,* an approx. 300km^2 rocky outcrop of large and small hills that shimmer in all colours *(from Coober Pedy or William Creek | A$320 | wrightsair.com.au).*

SIGHTSEEING

OLD TIMERS MINE

Tours are run to these former opal mines. Two dugout houses can also be visited. *Daily 9am–5pm | A$15 | Crowders Gully Road | cooberpedy. com/old-timers-mine*

EATING & DRINKING

OUTBACK BAR & GRILL

Service station, pub and restaurant in one. It might not sound inviting, but the burgers are the best in town. *Daily | 454 Hutchison Street | tel. 08 86 72 32 50 | $*

SHOPPING

Shops in Hutchison Street work opals and sell jewellery. Prices here are lower than in cities *(cooberpedy.com/ opals-2).* Check out *Opalios (8 Hutchison Street | opalios.com.au),* for example.

AROUND COOBER PEDY

⑨ THE KANKU BREAKAWAYS CONSERVATION PARK

32km / 30 mins from Coober Pedy by car

The hilly, sparsely vegetated area that glows in different colours depending on the position of the sun is north of Coober Pedy and is a popular film location. Panorama Hill for example played an important role in the action film *Mad Max,* that helped Mel Gibson to his international breakthrough in 1979. ⫐ *E5*

A GOOD NIGHT'S SLEEP

FIRE STATION OR VILLA?

The *North Adelaide Heritage Group (tel. 08 82 67 20 20 | adelaide heritage.com | $$$)* offers 19 different accommodation options in central and north Adelaide in historical properties. Make yourself at home in Adelaide's very first fire station or treat yourself to a stay in an old mansion.

SPEND THE NIGHT IN A MINE

Find out what it is like to live in a dugout at a disused opal mine. *Radeka's Dugout Backpackers (34 rooms | Oliver Road | tel. 08 86 72 52 23 | radekadownunder. com.au | $–$$),* in Coober Pedy, offer several options, from a reasonable bed in a shared room to an underground family suite.

TASMANIA

AUSTRALIA IN MINIATURE

To the rest of the country, Tasmania is that little island "under Down Under" where time somehow passes more slowly. Tasmanians, for their part, confidently call the Australian mainland "the North Island".

Despite its compact size, Tasmania has a lot to offer: almost one third of its countryside is a protected area – craggy mountain peaks, huge ferns, giant trees covered with moss, fast-flowing streams, lakes and hidden beaches. Then there are the stunning mountain

Dove Lake and Cradle Mountain

landscapes inland, edged by divine bays along the east coast.

Cut off from mainland Australia, plants and animals have evolved here that cannot be found anywhere else. The main island is about three times the size of Wales and is the smallest and coldest state in Australia. Most of the 520,000 or so inhabitants live in Hobart in the south and Launceston in the north. Tasmania can best be explored by hire car. In summer, accommodation should be booked in advance.

TASMANIA

Stanley

Smithton

Wynyard

Burnie

Devonpor
p. 163

Ridgley

Waratah

Sheffield

Zeehan

AUSTRALIA

INDIAN OCEAN

Queenstown

**Cradle Mountain-Lake St
Clair National Park ★**

Strahan ★
p. 165

300km, 4¼ hrs

Franklin-Gordon Wild Rivers National Park ★

MARCO POLO HIGHLIGHTS

★ **HOBART**
The Tasmanian capital enjoys a perfect mix
of mountains and coast ➤ p. 158

★ **PORT ARTHUR**
Ruins with a gruesome past, surrounded
by delightful scenery ➤ p. 159

★ **FREYCINET NATIONAL PARK**
Queen Elizabeth II herself soaked up the
view at Wineglass Bay with its secluded
beaches ➤ p. 162

★ **CRADLE MOUNTAIN–LAKE ST CLAIR
NATIONAL PARK**
Virtually untouched mountain landscapes
with superb hiking trails ➤ p. 164

★ **STRAHAN**
Fishing village and the gateway to
Tasmania's wilderness ➤ p. 165

★ **FRANKLIN-GORDON WILD RIVERS
NATIONAL PARK**
Jungle expedition by boat ➤ p. 165

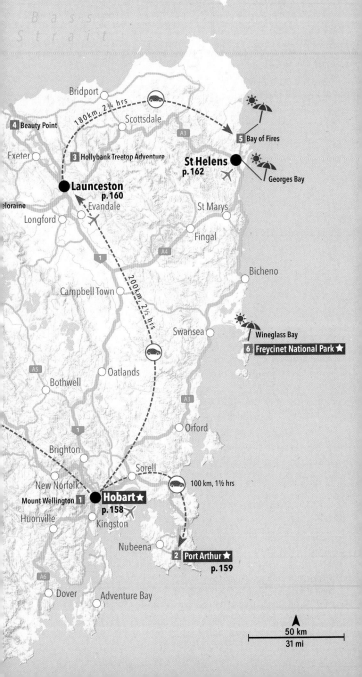

B a s s
S t r a i t

Bridport

180 km, 2¾ hrs

Scottsdale

A3

4 Beauty Point

Exeter

3 Hollybank Treetop Adventure

5 Bay of Fires

St Helens
p. 162

Launceston
p. 160

Evandale

Georges Bay

Deloraine

St Marys

Longford

Fingal

1

A4

200 km, 2½ hrs

Campbell Town

Bicheno

Swansea

Wineglass Bay

6 Freycinet National Park ★

Oatlands

A5

Bothwell

A3

Orford

1

Brighton

Sorell

New Norfolk

100 km, 1½ hrs

Mount Wellington 1

Hobart ★
p. 158

Huonville

Kingston

Nubeena

2 Port Arthur ★
p. 159

A6

Dover

Adventure Bay

50 km
31 mi

HOBART

(□ H8) **Mountains, bush and bays: romantic ★ Hobart (pop. 220,000), with its well-preserved colonial buildings, nestles among spectacular mountain ranges and the deep-blue Derwent River.**

The centre of activity is the unbelievably pretty, natural harbour of *Sullivans Cove*. On a clear day, the views from *Mount Wellington* are beyond compare.

SIGHTSEEING

BATTERY POINT

Tiny historical workers' houses with front gardens full of flowers, old sandstone villas, independent cafés, bookshops and antique shops are features of Hobart's oldest area around Hampden Road. Climb the old stone Kellys Steps from Salamanca Place to Battery Point and stroll to Arthurs Circus, the old village square. Hampden Road has some lovely cafés as well as the small ☛ *Narryna Heritage Museum (Tue–Sun 10am–4pm, daily in summer | admission free | tmag.tas.gov.au | ⊙ 30 mins).*

MONA (MUSEUM OF OLD AND NEW ART) ⫢

A machine that digests food like a human body and 150 reproductions of the female reproductive organs – in porcelain. Call that art? This private underground collection *(Wed–Mon 10am–5pm | A$28 | ⊙ 2 hrs)* belonging to an eccentric multi-millionaire is

WHERE TO START?

Sullivans Cove, where tourist boats and ferries come in, is a good place to start a stroll around the city centre and the historical districts of Salamanca Place and Battery Point. If you arrive by bus, get off at Franklin Square/Elizabeth Street, not far from the Travel Centre.

as famous as it is provocative. And yet it catapulted Hobart onto the world's modern art stage overnight. The complex also includes a brewery, Moo Brew, a wine cellar and bar, and an elegant restaurant, *The Source (Wed–Mon, Wed–Sat until 6pm | $$$).* You can also get there by boat *(from Brook St Ferry Terminal/Sullivans Cove)* | *655 Main Road | Berriedale | mona.net.au*

EATING & DRINKING

BLUE EYE

Small restaurant serving fresh seafood. Enjoy Tasmanian wines and a view out over the hustle and bustle of Salamanca Place. *Daily | Castray Esplanade/Salamanca Place | tel. 03 62 23 52 97 | blueeye.net.au | $$$*

FISH FRENZY

An institution which always serves wonderfully fresh seafood. *Daily | Elizabeth Street Pier | tel. 03 62 31 21 34 | fishfrenzy.com.au | $$–$$$*

JACKMAN & MCROSS

This bustling bakery is great for a

coffee break or breakfast. *57 Hampden Road | Battery Point*

MURES

This restaurant has its own fleet of fishing boats. Guests can choose between the elegant dining room on the first floor *($$–$$$)*, a self-service area on the ground floor *($–$$)* and a sushi bar *($$–$$$)*. *Daily | Victoria Dock | Sullivans Cove | tel. 03 62 31 20 09 | mures.com.au*

SPORT & ACTIVITIES

Premier Travel Tasmania (tel. 03 62 31 42 14 | premiertraveltasmania. com) organises very good tours lasting one or several days (from A$340) for groups of two or more people, with a special emphasis on watching wildlife and exploring the natural beauty of Tasmania.

NIGHTLIFE

Late in the afternoon on Fridays, you can enjoy live music at ☛ *Rektango (5.30–7.30pm)* in the courtyard of historic Salamanca Place – absolutely free of charge.

AROUND HOBART

◼ MOUNT WELLINGTON

17km / 25 mins from Hobart by car
Make sure to take a jacket, because a cold wind can blow up here even on

Early European settlers thought the wombat was a type of badger

summer days. Going "up" is a must, because the view over Hobart – and on a clear day even as far Bruny Island – is simply unbeatable. You can drive to the top. If you prefer to hike, take the two- to three-hour *Organ Pipes Walk*, which leads from The Springs to the giant stone pillars dotted along the mountains. The views out over the city are incredible. *⌂ H8*

INSIDER TIP
Organ pipes in the mountains

◻ PORT ARTHUR ★

100km / 1 hr 30 mins from Hobart by car
It might by 150 years since the last unfortunate prisoners served their penance here, but you'll still feel goosebumps amongst these old ruins on a peninsula south of Hobart,

especially if you join one of the guided tours *(daily 9am–5pm | from A$39 including Harbour Cruise | port arthur.org.au)*. Allow at least four hours for this experience, ideally in the early afternoon. Or you can meet the local ghosts on the 90-minute *Ghost Tour (A$27)* in the evening.

Admittedly, it can get quite rough on the three-hour boat trips from Port Arthur along the cliffs. However, these excursions are not to be missed, because you'll have the chance to observe animals and to see Australia's highest rock needles rising out of the water *Tasman Island Cruises (A$135 | tel. 03 62 50 22 00 | tasmancruises. com.au)*. About 10km from Port Arthur, on the junction to Koonya is the *Tasmanian Devil Unzoo (daily 9am–5pm | A$35 | Port Arthur Highway | Taranna | tasmaniandevil unzoo.com.au)*, which is great for watching Tasmanian devils. *H8*

LAUNCESTON

(H8) **Tasmania's second largest city (pop. 84,000) is a very popular gourmet destination.**

You don't just get to visit the many good restaurants but also the vineyards and fruit plantations in nearby Tamar Valley. Numerous historical buildings and parks can be found in Launceston city centre.

SIGHTSEEING

CATARACT GORGE

The deep gorge of the fast-flowing *South Esk River* reaches right into the heart of the city. A walk that lasts around one hour takes you across the swaying Alexandra suspension bridge up to the steep *Eagle Eyrie Lookout* and on to the old *Toll House on Kings* Bridge. A one-hour boat trip with *Tamar River Cruises (daily 9.30am–3.30pm | A$33 | Home Point Cruise Terminal, at the end of Home Point Parade | tel. 03 63 34 99 00 | tamarrivercruises.com.au)* through the dramatic rocky gorge is equally enticing.

EATING & DRINKING

PIPER'S BROOK VINEYARD

Lunch surrounded by vineyards can be enjoyed in a number of wineries north of Launceston. Piper's Brook Vineyard has great food and lovely views from the terrace. *Daily 11am–4pm | 1216 Pipers Brook Road | kreglingerwineestates.com | $–$$*

STILLWATER

This trendy bistro serves award-winning cuisine. *Daily | 2 Bridge Road | tel. 03 63 31 41 53 | $$$*

THREE STEPS ON GORGE

Australian pub classics like steak or fish and chips are on the menu at this old hotel. Live music often adds to the great atmosphere. *Daily | 158 Gorge Street | tel. 03 63 34 20 84 | $$*

A popular alternative to hiking is a boat trip through Cataract Gorge

AROUND LAUNCESTON

3 HOLLYBANK TREETOP ADVENTURE

20km / 20 mins from Launceston by car

This adrenalin-kick zipline adventure at a dizzying height is undiluted, action-packed, outdoor fun. Attached to ropes, participants 'fly' over distances of up to 370m. *Night flights* take place in the dark. *Daily 9am–5pm | 3 hrs incl. briefing approx. A$125 | 66 Hollybank Road | Underwood | treetopsadventure. au | ▢ H8*

INSIDER TIP Zip along

4 BEAUTY POINT

50km / 45 mins from Launceston by car

Three attractions await day trippers here on the western bank of the Tamar River that is quite wide at this point. At the *Platypus House (daily 10am–3.30pm | A$25 | platypushouse. com.au | ⏲ 2 hrs)*, you can also see the shy echidna, and at neighbouring *Seahorse World (daily 9.30am–4pm | A$22 | seahorseworld.com.au | ⏲ 1.5 hrs)* you can observe these tiny little creatures up close. To the south-west at *Beaconsfield*, the *Mine and Heritage Centre (daily from 9.30am–4.30pm | A$15 | West Street | beaconsfieldheritage.com.au | ⏲ 1 hr)* offers exciting insights into the history of Tasmania's biggest goldmine. *▢ H8*

Wineglass Bay

ST HELENS

(▯ H8) **This former whaling station in the east has become a lively, cheerful holiday resort (pop. 2,100) in protected Georges Bay.**

There is a good selection of accommodation and restaurants, plus the tranquil 🐾 *Georges Bay*, where you can safely swim.

AROUND ST HELENS

5 BAY OF FIRES 🐾

27km / 40 mins from St. Helens by car

This elongated bay to the north has fabulous, secluded, snowy-white beaches. En route, be sure to turn off to *Binalong Bay (binalongbay.com.au)* – even if you only stop for a snack and a creamy cappuccino on the panoramic terrace of the *Lichen Cafe (Main Road | tel. 03 63 76 80 86 | $$)*. Some wildly romantic campsites offer accommodation right beside the sea, although there is no electricity. ▯ H8

> **INSIDER TIP**
> Café with a view

6 FREYCINET NATIONAL PARK ⭐

120km / 1 hr 30 mins from St Helens by car

Protected countryside with secluded sandy beaches – the one in 🐾 *Wineglass Bay* is considered one of the loveliest in the world, and it's most certainly worth the approximately three-hour walk from the car park and back. There are wonderful views of the coast from the water, either on a four-hour *Eco Cruise (A$150 | tel. 03 62 57 03 55 | wineglassbay cruises.com.au)* in a sleek catamaran, or – if you want something a little sportier – in a kayak from *Freycinet Adventures (A$105) | tel. 03 62 57 05 00 | freycinetadventures. com.au)*. ▯ H8

DEVONPORT

(□ H8) **Devonport (pop. 30,500) is the gateway to Tasmania's rugged northwest.**

Daily car ferries from Melbourne dock in the town's port. From Mersey Bluff with its lighthouse you can look along the coast as far as Burnie on a clear day.

EATING & DRINKING

MRS JONES RESTAURANT

The best dishes on the international menu are prepared using fresh local ingredients and are served on the top floor of the surf club with views of the water. Do try the tempura oysters! *Closed Mon & Tue | Williams Street/ corner Bluff Road | tel. 03 64 23 38 81 | mrsjonesrbl.com.au | $$$*

AROUND DEVONPORT

7 DELORAINE

54km / 40 mins from Devonport by car

For gourmets, this rural town to the south-east is well worth a detour. The salmon farm 41° *South (6km further south-west | signposted on the Montana Road | 41southtasmania. com),* farms this delicious fish without the use of any chemicals. The small shop sells fresh salmon, smoked products and salmon paste. And if you fancy something sweet, head for *Honey Farm (39 Sorell Street | approx. 20km west, in Chudleigh | melitahoneyfarm.com.au).* The star among the many types of honey is the aromatic *leatherwood honey* from the pollen of local giant trees. □ *H8*

8 STANLEY

125km / 1 hr 30 mins from Devonport by car

Victorian houses and small shops line the old main street in Stanley (pop. 540) below *The Nut (Circular Head).* The steep rock is a popular place for sightseers. The hike up takes 10–20 minutes, and you'll be rewarded with a lovely circular walk (approx. 30 minutes) around the top. A little easier and just as scenic is the chairlift *(daily 9.30am–5pm | return A$17 | thenutchairlift.com.au).*

Penguins and colonies of sea lions can be visited on the coast or else take a boat trip *(75 mins | A$55 | tel. 03 64 58 12 94 | stanleysealcruises.com. au).* If you're feeling peckish, *Stanley's Hotel (daily | 15 Wharf Road | tel. 03 64 58 11 61 | stanleyvillage.com.au | $$)* and *Xanders (evenings only, closed Mon & Tue | 25 Church Street | tel. 03 64 58 12 22 | $$-$$$)* are truly outstanding restaurants. □ *G8*

CRADLE MOUNTAIN-LAKE ST CLAIR NP

(🔲 G8) ★ **Cradle Mountain-Lake St Clair National Park combines a rough, mountain landscape with peaceful mountain lakes and numerous hiking paths.**

There are two entrances: in the south, Highway A10 turns off to Lake St Clair; in the north, a side road takes you to Cradle Valley. The latter has turned into a kind of centre for the park, with an infrastructure tailored to tourists' needs, whereas Lake St Clair boasts an untouched, romantic and peaceful shoreline. You'll need to purchase a park pass (*A$17/person or A$60/car*).

EATING & DRINKING

HIGHLAND RESTAURANT

This renowned restaurant complete with wood-burning stove is as rustic as it is chic. Plus, it's part of the comfortable *Cradle Mountain Lodge,* where you can relax with a spa treatment and stay overnight. *Daily | tel. 13 00 80 61 92 | cradlemountainlodge.com.au | $$$*

SPORT & ACTIVITIES

CRADLE VALLEY BOARDWALK

There's a well-maintained trail from the *Interpretation Centre* in the *National Park Ranger Station* (which has a worthwhile natural history display, just inside the north entrance) and Dove Lake. The 17-km route there

Trekking through the rainforest in Cradle Mountain-Lake St Clair National Park

and back (walking time five hours) leads past scrub covered in moss and giant trees. If that's too far for you, you can take the shuttle bus from the *Visitor Centre*, which is free for guests with a parking pass.

OVERLAND TRACK

This trail from Cradle Mountain to Lake St Clair is around 65km long. Taking about five days, you will pass through mountainous areas, upland moor, rainforest and deep valleys with spectacular waterfalls. For information on guided tours *(from approx. A\$2,200)* see: *tasmanianexpeditions.com | Oct–May reservations obligatory | overlandtrack.com.au*

STRAHAN

(▢ G8) **Is this really what the end of the world looks like? The little port of ★ Strahan (pop. 700), with its pretty wooden houses, attracts around 25,000 visitors every year.**

This is due in the main to its wildly romantic location amongst impenetrable bush, and *Macquarie Harbour*, a natural harbour.

EATING & DRINKING

THE STRAHAN VILLAGE

A variety of good accommodation and two restaurants are available right on the harbour. *Daily | The Esplanade | tel. 03 64 71 42 00 | strahanvillage. com.au | \$\$–\$\$\$*

NIGHTLIFE

Entertainment with tradition: The Ship that Never Was is a humorous one-hour play about a successful escape from the penal colony. For some time now it has been enacted every day at around 5.30pm in the *Strahan Visitor Centre (ticket A\$25)*.

AROUND STRAHAN

9 FRANKLIN-GORDON WILD RIVERS NATIONAL PARK ★

The boats of *Gordon River Cruises (from A\$135 | 24 Esplanade | tel. 03 64 71 43 00 | gordonrivercruises.com. au)* sail from Macquarie Harbour along the Gordon and through one of the few jungles of this moderate zone with trees that are up to 2,000 years old. The tour lasts about six hours and you'll stop along the way at the former convict settlement of *Bonnet Island*. ▢ G8

10 QUEENSTOWN

40km / 45 mins from Strahan by car
This little mining town is located in the middle of a lunar landscape that is slowly being reafforested. Mainly copper and gold are mined here. The museum railway 🚉 *West Coast Wilderness Railway (1–6 times a week)* steams along an adventurous route between Queenstown and Strahan *(from A\$185 | wcwr.com.au)*. ▢ G8

DISCOVERY TOURS

Do you want to get under the skin of the country? Then our discovery tours provide the perfect guide – they include advice on which sights to visit, tips on where to stop for that perfect holiday snap, a choice of the best places to eat and drink, and suggestions for fun activities.

❶ SPECTACULAR COASTAL TRIP: GREAT OCEAN ROAD ⭐

- ➤ Surf where the world pros surf
- ➤ Paddle with platypuses
- ➤ Snap a selfie with the Twelve Apostles

📍	Melbourne	🏁	Flagstaff Hill Maritime Village
⏱	4 days	➡	572km
🚗	Driving time: 13 hrs		
ℹ	⓰ **Flagstaff Hill**: book tickets for the show in advance.		

Watch out for wildlife!

SURFING HIGHLIGHTS AT BELL'S BEACH

Highway M1 takes you from ❶ Melbourne ➤ p. 74 *to* ❷ Geelong. Visit the harbour town's Botanic Gardens and art deco seawater pool on the waterfront, plus the National Wool Museum *(Mon–Fri 9.30am–5pm, Sat & Sun from 10am | A\$9 | 26 Moorabool Street | geelongaustralia.com.au/nwm).*

From Geelong, follow the signs (B100) to ❸ Torquay. The settlement is considered the mecca of the surfing scene – as is confirmed by the Australian National Surfing Museum *(77 Beach Road | daily 9am–5pm | A\$12 | australiannationalsurfingmuseum.com.au).* The well-stocked surf shops in town have all the equipment you need, so you can hire a board and emulate the pros who congregate on Bells Beach for the international Rip Curl Pro Bells Beach at Easter. A signposted turning at the end of the town goes to the beach. Back on the Great Ocean Road, drive to your next beach delight: the tiny bathing resort of ❹ Anglesea, where *Harvey Street* has a lookout with fabulous views of the coast. *Another 14km,* and you'll come to ❺ Fairhaven Beach , another dream beach, and then to ❻ Lorne *(lornelink.com.au).* The lively tourist centre offers all sorts of food options,

DAY 1	
❶ **Melbourne**	
72km	1hr
❷ **Geelong**	
26km	45 mins
❸ **Torquay**	
20km	20 mins
❹ **Anglesea**	
14km	15 mins
❺ **Fairhaven Beach**	
16km	15 mins
❻ **Lorne**	
49km	45 mins

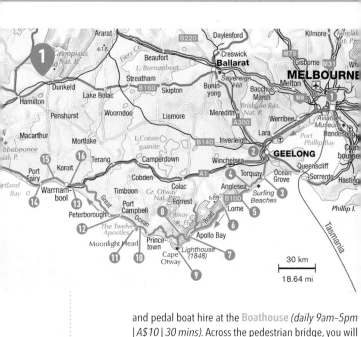

and pedal boat hire at the Boathouse *(daily 9am–5pm | A$10 | 30 mins)*. Across the pedestrian bridge, you will find freshly caught fish and seafood at The Pier Seafood *(daily | Lorne Pier Head | $$)*, which has a restaurant, snack bar and shop at the end of town. Now comes one of the loveliest sections of the Great Ocean Road. It's 49km to Apollo Bay ➤ p. 82, a very friendly holiday resort with the ❼ Marengo Holiday Park *(tel. 03 52 37 61 62 | marengopark.com.au | $$)* close to the beach with cabins and camping for overnight stays.

❼ Marengo Holiday Park

ON THE HUNT FOR PLATYPUSES

Now continue to the densely wooded wilderness of the Great Otway National Park ➤ p. 82. After only 15km, a sign on the roadside invites you to the (signposted) 40-minute circular ❽ Maits Rest Rainforest Walk. If this puts you in the mood for more: there are many charming hiking routes of varying lengths through the national park that are perfect for observing the animals Experience platypus close up on the guided paddle tour "Paddle with the Platypus" in the late afternoon with Otway Eco Tours *(3–4 hrs | approx. A$85 | tel. 04 19 67 09 85 | platypustours.net.au)*.

DAY 2

15km 20 mins

❽ Maits Rest Rainforest Walk

134km 4 hrs 30 mins

Back in the car, *follow the 13km turning to Cape Otway*, which is marked by the white ❾ Cape Otway Lighthouse *(daily 9.30am–4.30pm | A$20 | 2 rooms, 6 houses | tel. 03 52 37 92 40 | lightstation.com | $$$)*, built here on the steep coast by convicts in the middle of the 19th century. You can visit the historic site and spend the night, if you like.

SELFIES WITH THE SANDSTONE APOSTLES

The next stretch of Great Ocean Road is not particularly spectacular – until you get to Port Campbell National Park ➤ p. 83 and its Twelve Apostles. The first good views of the famous rock formation in the foaming waves are available from the ❿ Gibson Steps to the left of the road. In good weather, you can walk down to the eight remaining limestone stacks from here. *It's about 2km by car to the car park* and the ⓫ Twelve Apostles Lookout, from where you can look over the eroded rocks. *Drive past the Loch Ard Gorge* (be sure to stop!) to the fishing village of ⓬ Port Campbell, where you can end the day in one of the pleasant restaurants, such as Waves *(daily | 29 Lord Street | tel. 03 55 98 61 11 | $$)*. There are also cafés and a safe bathing beach in the middle. Accommodation is available at the Southern Ocean Motor Inn *(28 rooms | 2 Lord Street | tel. 03 55 98 62 31 | southernoceanmotorinn.com | $$)*.

❾ Cape Otway Lighthouse	

DAY 3	
76km	1 hr 30 mins

❿ Gibson Steps	
2km	10 mins

⓫ Twelve Apostles Lookout	
13km	25 mins

⓬ Port Campbell	

You can stay in the landmark lighthouse at Cape Otway

WHALES & DISASTERS

DAY 4

The last section of the panoramic route offers a final look at picturesque coastal formations such as the London Arch or *The Grotto*. *At Km13* the road passes the sandy Bay of Martyrs, where storm birds nest in the summer, and *20km further on* it merges with the *Princes Highway (A1) towards* Warrnambool. Today, this former whaling station attracts whale-watchers, because in the Australian winter (June–September) the southern right whales come here to calve and are easy to observe from the lookout platform on ⑬ Logans Beach *(Logans Beach Road turns off Hopkins Point Road)*.

71km 1 hr 25 mins
⑬ Logans Beach
33km 30 mins

For lunch, it's worth the drive along *Princes Highway to* ⑭ Port Fairy with its listed houses. On the way back stop off about halfway at the ⑮ Tower Hill State Game Reserve, where a fascinating wilderness with countless animals fills the deep crater of an extinct volcano. It is surrounded by a narrow road, where you must always be on the lookout to see wild animals crossing, especially from the late afternoon.

⑭ Port Fairy
17km 15 mins
⑮ Tower Hill State Game Reserve
16km 15 mins

Be sure to be back in Warrnambool in the evening, more precisely at the ⑯ Flagstaff Hill Maritime Village *(daily 9am–5pm | A$18, show A$26 | Merri Street | flagstaffhill.com)*, the reconstruction of a harbour town from the 19th century, for the sound and laser show "Shipwrecked", which brings to life the exciting story of Shipwreck Coast. For old-fashioned accommodation, look no further than the adjoining, prettily refurbished Lighthouse Lodge *(3 rooms | flagstaffhill.com | $–$$)*.

⑯ Flagstaff Hill Maritime Village

❷ A JOURNEY THROUGH DREAMTIME

➤ Take a 4x4 through the Red Centre
➤ Scramble to the crater's edge
➤ Sunset at Uluru

📍	Alice Springs	🏁	Uluru
🔄	3 days	➡	785km
🚗	Driving time: 12 hrs		

ℹ️ What to pack: insect protection, road maps, permit. You need a vehicle with four-wheel drive. Contact the Visitor Information Centre in ❶ **Alice Springs** for information on the current condition of unmade roads and the opening times of the service stations. Fill the car with petrol at the beginning of every day, and be sure to take plenty of drinking water and food with you. Some of the time you will be driving through Aboriginal land. You are not allowed to take alcohol with you. In order to drive the Mereenie Loop Road, you must purchase the *Mereenie Tour Pass ($5)* from the Visitor Information Centre in ❶ **Alice Springs**.

RED ROCK GORGE

The drive starts in ❶ Alice Springs ➤ p. 117. In the centre, *turn off Stuart Highway onto Larapinta Drive heading west. After 7km*, you'll see the grave site of John Flynn, the founder of Royal Flying Doctor Service ➤ p. 117, on the left side of the road. Take your first break at ❷ Simpsons Gap. It's a short walk through the eucalyptus trees to this waterhole. This place will help you to understand why the gorges of the MacDonnell Ranges are of economic as well as cultural importance to local Aboriginal people as they provided them with water and food. *24km further along Larapinta Drive, turn onto* ❸ Standley Chasm. The chasm is especially spectacular around midday, when the sun turns it into a glowing red corridor.

DER TIP
Lighting up

DAY 1
❶ **Alice Springs**
25km 40 mins

❷ **Simpsons Gap**
41km 1 hr

❸ **Standley Chasm**
60km 1 hr 25 mins

4 Ellery Creek Big Hole	
16km	45 mins

5 Serpentine Gorge	
16km	35 mins

6 Ochre Pits	
26km	45 mins

7 Ormiston Gorge	
12km	20 mins

8 Glen Helen Homestead Resort	

Back on Larapinta Drive, you'll leave the road to take Namatjira Drive along the West MacDonnell Ranges. The road ends at **4 Ellery Creek Big Hole**. The country side around this large waterhole is extremely varied and very interesting geologically – and perfect for a picnic. Another place on *Namatjira Drive* that is worth stopping at is **5 Serpentine Gorge**. As its name indicates, the gorge winds its way through the rock like a reptile.

EARTH HISTORY IN OCHRE

Afterwards, don't ignore the **6 Ochre Pits** as you drive past. They are a cross-section of the 700 million years of this region's geological history. The Western Arrernte people used the pale yellow to rust-red ochre colouring for their rock paintings. After a final stop at **7 Ormiston Gorge**, you'll arrive at **8 Glen Helen Homestead Lodge** *(25 rooms, campsite | Namatjira Drive | tel. 08 89 56 72 08 | glenhelen.com.au | $$)*. Nearby is Finke River, which is considered to be the oldest river in the world, and is also a haven for birds.

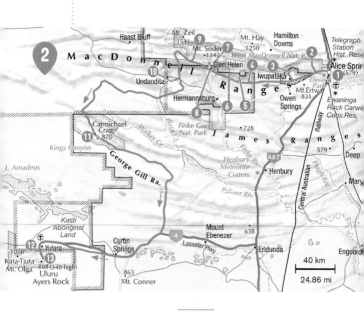

CRATER HIKE

Namatjira Drive is now a dirt track, and will take you through the fresh morning air to idyllic ❾ Redbank Gorge, before you *change direction to the south-west* and the Tnorala Conservation Reserve with the ❿ Gosses Bluff Crater, which is the result of a meteorite impact about 140 million years ago and is worshipped by the Western Arrernte people as a holy site. If the very bumpy *10-km gravel road* doesn't bother you, you'll get to a dead end in the vast crater of 5-km diameter. The silence when you turn off the engine is unbelievable. A *signposted hiking path* takes you even closer to the crater.

You still have about 180km of gravel road to travel to the Watarrka National Park/Kings Canyon. At the next junction, turn right onto Mereenie Loop Road (permit required), and from now on you'll be travelling across Aboriginal land. The best options for accommodation, including a campsite and views of an amazing starry sky, are available at ⓫ Kings Canyon ➤ p. 118.

ULURU AT DUSK

An approximately two- to three-hour walk will take you through the canyon in the morning and to the made-up route *along Luritja Road, where you turn right onto Lasseter Highway* to Uluru. Plan the day so that you have enough time to check in at the ⓬ Ayers Rock Resort (Yulara) ➤ p. 120 before sunset *(sunset times: short.travel/aus1)* to take up your position on ⓭ Uluru ➤ p. 119.

Kings Canyon

DAY 2	
26km	50 mins
❾ Redbank Gorge	
52km	1 hr 15 mins
❿ Gosses Bluff Crater	
182km	3 hrs 10 mins
⓫ Kings Canyon	

DAY 3	
307km	6 hrs
⓬ Ayers Rock Resort (Yulara)	
22km	1 hr 30 mins
⓭ Uluru	

❸ RAINFOREST HIKE IN LAMINGTON NATIONAL PARK

➤ Powerful waterfalls
➤ A stop in the eucalyptus forest
➤ View over the rainforest

📍 Car park,
Binna Burra

🏁 Car park,
Binna Burra

🔄 7–8 hrs

⇄ 16km

🚶 Walking time: 5½ hrs

↗ Height: 680m

▂▃▅ Difficulty: easy

What to pack: insect protection, drinking water (at least 1.5 litres/person), hiking map.

ℹ Up-to-date information on the accessibility of the trail is available from the ranger (*Mon–Fri 1.30–3.30pm, Sat & Sun 9am–5pm | tel. 07 55 33 35 84*) or at s*hort.travel/aus2.*
To get to the ❶ **car park** in Binna Burra, follow Binna Burra Road to its end.

FROM WATERFALL TO WATERFALL …

❶ Binna Burra car park

5km — 1 hr 30 mins

You start at the top: the ❶ car park in Binna Burra is already at an altitude of 800m. *First of all, follow the Border Track.* The well-constructed track is basically the main artery in the dense network of hiking trails in the national park. Behind towering evergreen brush box trees *turn onto the Coomera Falls Circuit and enjoy a gentle stroll down.*

❷ Coomera Falls Lookout

100m — 5 mins

The route becomes steeper towards the ❷ Coomera Falls Lookout, where you will have impressive waterfall views right in front of you – and your camera lens. Time for a break! Coomera River plunges 64m, while the nearby Yarrabilgong Falls drop an impressive 160m. In view of the sparkling surroundings, it's hardly surprising that the air is so wonderfully fresh. But be careful if it rains: it's easy to lose your footing on the slippery ground!

You'll soon leave the thicket behind you on the ascending path, and arrive at the lighter eucalyptus forest. Allow yourself a rest on the edge of the 160-m-deep ❸ Coomera River Gorge and let the spectacular surroundings work their magic on you.

... AND BANK TO BANK

You'll soon cross the Coomera River for the first time. Keep your hiking boots on because of the leeches, even though insect repellent is supposed to keep these harmless but tiresome bloodsuckers at bay. *You'll change banks a number of times over the next 3.5km, past the* Bahnamboola Falls, Gwongarragong Falls *and* Chigigunya Falls, *to name but a few* of the now-frequent waterfalls. The *blue Lamington spiny crayfish* is at home in the numerous water-filled rock pools.

By the time you get to the ❹ Goorawa Falls, *where the path rejoins the Border Track,* you'll have managed more than half of the route – and will have earned your-self another stop (for lunch). *From now on, follow the route to the north – and uphill: you have about 100m to climb.*

At the top, Antarctic beech forest is a key feature of the vegetation: a woodland that only survives in cooler climates on this continent. In clear weather, there are wonderful views over the gorges of the high plateau, e.g. from ❺ Joahla Lookout, before the Border Track takes you back to the ❶ car park in Binna Burra.

❸ Coomera River gorge	
3.5 km	1 hr
❹ Goorawa Falls	
3km	1 hr

❺ Joahla Lookout	
4.5 km	1 hr 15 mins
❶ Binna Burra car park	

GOOD TO KNOW
HOLIDAY BASICS

ARRIVAL

GETTING THERE

Flights from London to the east coast of Australia take 23+ hours. The long journey is more pleasant if you stop over in Singapore or Hong Kong (from London approx. 15 hours, on to Sydney eight hours), for example. Depending on the time of year, an economy class return ticket from London can cost anything from around £900/US$1,400 upwards. Cathay Pacific also offers a comfortable and attractively priced premium economy class. Don't forget, when comparing prices, to check whether taxes and other fees are included. Some airlines such as Qantas (*qantas.com.au*) and Cathay Pacific (*cathaypacific.com/en*) offer cheap or free tickets for domestic flights within Australia when you purchase an international ticket.

GETTING IN

To enter Australia you'll need a free tourist visa that can usually be issued or applied for when purchasing a plane ticket (eVisitor visa). It is valid for a stay of up to three months. It is strictly forbidden to take paid employment of any kind and failing to observe this law could result in a heavy fine. People between 18 and 31 years of age may apply for a special working-holiday-travel visa valid for up to two years, which allows them to accept temporary employment (*immi.homeaffairs.gov.au/visas*). Information: *Australian High Commission | Strand, London WC2B 4LA | tel. 020 7379 4334 | uk.embassy. gov.au*).

An Instagram moment on the Stuart Highway, which links north and south

 Time difference: +8 / +9½ / +10 hrs

There are three time zones in Australia.

Western Australia: Western Standard Time (GMT +8 hours)

Northern Territory and South Australia: Central Standard Time (GMT +9.5 hours)

Other states: Eastern Standard Time (GMT +10 hours).

Daylight Saving time in most states (except Queensland, Northern Territory and Western Australia) is between the first Sunday in October and the first Sunday in April.

CLIMATE & WHEN TO GO

The southeast (New South Wales, Tasmania, Victoria and South Australia), as well as Western Australia south of the Tropic of Capricorn, are best visited between October and April (spring and summer). Queensland, Northern Territory and the north of Western Australia are best visited between April and November (the dry season). At other times of the year it is generally cool in the south, and hot and sticky in the north (north of the Tropic of Capricorn) – and it can rain very heavily. For current weather information go to bom.gov.au.

Accommodation, and campsites in particular, are often fully booked during the summer holidays in December and January and over long weekends. What's more, prices can double or even triple at these times.

Adapter Type I

The mains voltage is 240 volt a.c. Most standard European devices operate without any problem but you do need an adapter, available for example at airports, luggage shops or chemists. Visitors from Canada and the US may need a voltage converter.

GETTING AROUND

CAR HIRE

If you want to see more than the standard tourist highlights along the coasts, it's a good idea to hire a car. Small hire cars are often more reasonable than in Europe (from approx. A$25/day without insurance), and diesel and petrol are also cheaper (A$1.20–1.60/litre). For a price comparison go to *vroomvroomvroom.com. au.*

If you want to save money or like being outdoors, book a camper van (from approx. A$50/day without insurance). Whether you need a four-wheel-drive or not obviously depends on the route you're planning. Make sure your car hire company permits off-road driving *(on unsurfaced/gravel roads)* and take out a fully comprehensive insurance without co-payment. Be careful about supplements, for example if you plan to drop the car in a different city, or extra charges for

credit card payments. An international driving licence is obligatory for some companies. The best offers for campervans can be found online. Major hire companies include *Maui (maui.com. au), Apollo (apollocamper.com)* and *Kea (keacampers.com).*

The Australians drive on the left and give way to traffic coming from the right. In general, the speed limit in a built-up area is 30 or 40mph, outside towns it's 60mph, and 70mph on motorways (80mph in Northern Territory). True motorways can only be found in Australia near major cities. Many highways are in fact single-lane country roads with occasional overtaking lanes.

INTERCITY BUSES

With the exception of the East Coast, Australia's bus and rail network is quite sparse. It is often a good idea to buy bus passes for intercity journeys before starting your journey. Such passes either allow you to make an unlimited number of stops on any chosen route, are divided into categories according to distance, or give you a reduction of 50%. The market is dominated by *Greyhound (greyhound. com.au).* An overview of a wide range of traffic connections is available at *buslines.com.au.*

INTERCITY TRAINS

The absolute best way to grasp the simply enormous scale of this continent is on the intercity *Indian Pacific (sleeper cabins from A$2,100),* which runs from Sydney via Adelaide and the Nullarbor Plain to Perth. The whole

FESTIVALS & EVENTS
ALL YEAR ROUND

JANUARY
Sydney Festival *sydneyfestival.org.au*
Mona Foma (Hobart): Tasmania's biggest cultural festival; *mofo.net.au*

FEBRUARY
Gay and Lesbian Mardi Gras (Sydney), *mardigras.org.au*
Perth International Arts Festival *perthfestival.com.au*
White Night Melbourne Artistic lighting concepts make the city glow; *whitenightmelbourne.com.au* (photo)

MARCH/APRIL
Rip Curl Pro (Torquay): International surfing competition; *ripcurl.com.au*

JUNE
Dark Mofo (Hobart): Music and art celebrate the winter solstice; *dark mofo.net.au*

JULY
Mowanjum Festival (Derby): Local Aboriginal artists showcase their work; *mowanjumarts.com/festival*

Lion's Camel Cup (Alice Springs) *camelcup.com.au*

AUGUST
Henley on Todd Regatta (Alice Springs): Surely the weirdest "regatta" in the world; *henleyontodd.com.au*
Festival of Darwin, *darwinfestival.org.au*

SEPTEMBER
Australian Football Grand Finale (Melbourne); *afl.com.au*
Shinju Matsuri (Broome): A festival celebrating pearls; *shinjumatsuri.com.au*

NOVEMBER
Melbourne Cup The race that brings the whole continent to a standstill; *flemington.com.au*

DECEMBER
Sydney to Hobart Yacht Race (Hobart); *rolexsydneyhobart.com*

trip takes three days, departing from Sydney on Wednesdays and Perth on Sundays. Other intercity trains run from Adelaide through the Red Centre to Darwin *(The Ghan)* and between Melbourne and Adelaide *(The Overland)*. Limited seats mean train trips should be organised as early as possible. Information and booking: *Great Southern Rail (tel. 08 82 13 44 01 | greatsouthernrail.com. au)*.

INTERNAL FLIGHTS

Competition among budget airlines is huge: *Jetstar (jetstar.com)*, *Virgin Australia (virginaustralia.com)*, *Tiger Air (tigerair.com.au)*. Prices for inland flights vary considerably. The earlier you book, the better for your holiday fund. *Regional Express (rex.com.au)* also flies to remote regions.

EMERGENCIES

EMERGENCY CALLS

Emergencies (tel. 000). Callers must then specify which service they require: fire, police or ambulance.

CONSULATES & EMBASSIES
BRITISH HIGH COMMISSION

Commonwealth Avenue | Canberra | ACT 2600 | tel. +61 2 62 70 66 66 (general enquiries) | ukinaustralia.fco. gov.uk
Apart from the High Commission, the United Kingdom has nine other offices in Australia, including the British Consulate-General in Sydney.

BRITISH CONSULATE-GENERAL

Level 16, Gateway Building | 1 Macquarie Place | Sydney | NSW 2000 | tel. +61 2 92 47 75 21 | ukinaustralia. fco.gov.uk/en. The website has information on other locations.

EMBASSY OF THE UNITED STATES OF AMERICA

Moonah Place | Yarralumla | Canberra | ACT 2600 | tel. +61 2 62 14 56 00 | canberra.usembassy.gov/contact.html.

HEALTH

UK and Irish citizens, and those from several other European nations, are entitled to free reciprocal Medicare treatment in Australian hospitals and at GPs, although there are certain restrictions. It is best to familiarise yourself beforehand with the conditions of the reciprocal arrangement as it does not, for example, cover private hospitals which can be very expensive. It is worth looking into the cost of additional health insurance before your journey. Most hospitals offer an interpreting service for foreign patients or the victims of accidents.

ESSENTIALS

ACCOMMODATION/CAMPING

Hotels in major cities are expensive *(A\$140–280 for 3- to 4-star hotels)*; flats/apartments are often a better alternative: they are bigger, better equipped and slightly cheaper. There is also a good choice of holiday homes for rent *(stayz.com.au)*. Outside urban centres there are numerous motels (A$90-150). Campsites (gosee australia.com.au | campsaustraliawide. com, also lists free sites) often have cabins and motel rooms (A$70-140). B&B is also popular (australianbedand breakfast.com.au), as is a stay on a station, as farms in Australia are called (farmstaycampingaustralia.com.au). Good accommodation can be found at short notice at wotif.com.au and ozbargain.com.au. Youth hostels and backpacker hostels – of which there are many – also have cheap double rooms. Rooms or even houses available privately can be found under airbnb.com.au, homestayweb.com and couchsurfing.org.

ALCOHOL

You have to be 18 to consume alcohol. Many towns and cities have designated dry zones – parks and beach sections where no alcohol may be consumed. It is strictly forbidden to take alcohol into Aboriginal territories even if asked to do so.

BANK HOLIDAYS

1 Jan	New Year
26 Jan	Australia Day
29 March 2024, 18 April 2025	Good Friday
1 April 2024, 21 April 2025	Easter Monday
25 April	Anzac Day
14 Nov	King's birthday
25/26 Dec	Christmas

BRING YOUR OWN

Bring your own or BYO on the front door of a restaurant means they don't serve wine – instead you get to bring your own. Buy it in the nearest bottleshop, often attached to pubs. The restaurant opens and refrigerates the bottles and charges a small fee, corkage (approx. A$5–8 per bottle).

CURRENCY

The unit of currency is the Australian dollar (A$). There are 5, 10, 20, 50 and 100 Australian dollar notes; 1 and 2 dollar coins; and 5, 10, 20 and 50 cent coins. Prices for goods and services are comparable to those in Britain. Some food is slightly more expensive. For the current exchange rate, see xe.com.

CUSTOMS

It is forbidden to import fruit, vegetables or meat into Australia due to the risk of disease. You may bring in 50 cigarettes or 50g of tobacco and 2.25 litres of alcohol per person duty-free, as well as personal items and gifts up to a value of A$900.

For purchases of more than A$300 in a shop in Australia you can reclaim the 10% VAT at the airport when you depart. You must however show the bill and items purchased at customs (customs.gov.au).

INTERNET & WIFI

Australia has good internet connections, especially in towns and cities. Almost every pub offers free WiFi. Some guesthouses and hotels may charge between A$3 and $10 per day, but WiFi is usually included in the price of your accommodation. There are also plenty of hotspots in the towns and cities (short.travel/aus31) where you

INSIDER TIP
Free internet

can access the internet free of charge. The local libraries offer internet access, and often computers as well for you to use for a specific length of time.

MONEY

Money can be changed, cash obtained from ATMs with bank and credit cards, and traveller's checks cashed without any problem at banks in major cities and tourist centres (opening times generally Mon–Fri 9am–4pm). Credit cards (especially Visa and MasterCard) are widely accepted. That said, it's still worth having cash in the outback.

HOW MUCH DOES IT COST?

Coffee	£2.50
	for a cappuccino
Beer	£4.25
	for a pint in a pub
Fast food	£5
	for a meal and soft drink
Petrol	£0.75
	for a litre of regular
Cinema	£10.15
	for a ticket
Surfboard	£13.50
	for 2 hrs' rental

OPENING HOURS

Restaurants, pubs, food shops and information offices in the larger towns are generally open every day. In cities, supermarkets are usually open from around 7am to 10pm, sometimes with shorter hours at weekends. Shops in shopping centres usually open from 9am to 5pm and until 8 or 9pm

RESPONSIBLE TRAVEL

Are you aware of your carbon footprint while travelling? You can offset your emissions (myclimate. org), plan your route with the environment in mind (routerank.com) and go gently on both nature and culture. If you would like to find out more about ecotourism please visit: ecotourism.org

on Thursdays. However, in the country, shops and restaurants are often closed over the weekend. And in the outback, some service stations, motels and small restaurants often close in the early evening.

POST

A postcard or a letter to Europe costs A$3 and takes about two weeks to arrive. Further information: auspost. com.au

PHONE & MOBILE PHONES

The international dialling code for Australia is 61, followed by the area code without the 0, i.e. 2 for Sydney (02). From Australia, the dialling code is 00 11 +44 for the UK, 00 11 +1 for the USA and Canada. Toll-free numbers start with 1800; six-digit numbers that start with 1300 are charged as local calls.

Prepaid cards for mobile phones for use in Australia can be bought before your journey for a set fee that normally includes a number of free calls and data for a set period. If you are staying longer in Australia, it's best to get an

Australian sim card, e.g. from Optus, Vodafone or Telstra. The best network in Australia is *Telstra (telstra.com.au)*. Satellite telephones are an alternative for use in the outback. These can also be rented, with prepaid credit *(e.g. trtelecom.com)*.

SMOKING

Smoking in, and in the vicinity of, all outdoor eating areas is not allowed. Many of the beaches and most pedestrian zones are also non-smoking. Violations are punished with high fines.

TOURIST INFORMATION

Tourism Australia *(australia.com)*; Tourism New South Wales *(visit nsw.com)*; Tourism Queensland *(queensland.com)*; Tourism Northern Territory *(tourismnt.com.au)*; Tourism Western Australia *(westernaustralia. com)*; Tourism South Australia *(south australia.com)*; Tourism Tasmania *(tourismtasmania.com.au)*.

WEATHER IN SYDNEY

■ High season
▦ Low season

	JAN	FEB	MARCH	APRIL	MAY	JUNE	JULY	AUG	SEPT	OCT	NOV	DEC
Daytime temperature	26°	26°	24°	22°	19°	16°	16°	17°	19°	22°	23°	25°
Night-time temperature	18°	18°	17°	14°	11°	9°	8°	9°	11°	13°	16°	17°
☀	7	7	6	5	5	4	5	6	6	7	7	7
🌧	7	8	8	7	5	9	5	7	7	9	8	8
≋	23	24	23	20	18	18	16	17	18	19	19	21

☀ Hours of sunshine per day   🌧 Rainy days per month   ≋ Sea temperature in °C

Aerial view of Sydney's Royal Botanic Gardens

HOLIDAY VIBES

FOR RELAXATION & CHILLING

FOR BOOKWORMS & FILM BUFFS

📖 DOWN UNDER
As usual you're guaranteed to laugh out loud while reading American journalist Bill Bryson's travel experiences in Australia (2001).

📷 RABBIT-PROOF FENCE
A moving insight into the tragic story of the *Stolen Generation*: forcibly separated from their parents, three girls dare to escape from the "Native Settlement" and make the long, uncertain journey home (2002).

📖 TRACKS
Back in the late 1970s, Australian Robyn Davidson flew to world fame when she set out alone with a dog and four camels on the 2,700-km journey from Alice Springs to the West Coast (1980).

📷 THE CASTLE
THE Australian classic. It might not offer action-packed plot twists, but this film keeps its audience spellbound throughout and, above all, makes them laugh (1997).

PLAYLIST
ON THE ROAD AGAIN

0:58

II COLD CHISEL – KHE SANH
One of the most Australian songs of all time.

▶ INXS – NEVER TEAR US APART
Australian rock legend Michael Hutchence and band still make our playlist.

▶ POWDERFINGER – SUNSET
The soundtrack for a road trip along the Australian coast.

▶ MIDNIGHT OIL – DIESEL AND DUST (ALBUM)
Peter Garrett was not just a minister, but a singer too.

▶ PAUL KELLY – EVERY FUCKING CITY
Songs with a whole load of empathy and even more Aussie humour.

▶ YOTHU YINDI – TREATY
This band mixes Aboriginal music traditions with rock band sounds

The holiday soundtrack is available on **Spotify** under **MARCO POLO** Australia

Or scan this code with the Spotify app

ONLINE

ABORIGINAL VISIT
diversetravel.com.au provides tours that give an excellent insight into Aboriginal Australian cultures.

EAT LIKE A KING
agfg.com.au is up to date with the best restaurants and cafés.

KIP IN THE OUTBACK
Where better to experience the outback than on a remote farm or in a secret caravan park? *outbackbeds.com.au* lists unique spots to stay overnight.

LEARN TO SPEAK AUSSIE
Want to speak like the locals? Check out the podcasts at *theaussieenglish podcast.com* or join an online lesson.

TRAVEL REPORTS
"70 best Australian travel blogs and websites": blog.feedspot.com/australia_travel_blog.

WHAT'S THE WEATHER LIKE?
Reliable source for weather forecasts and weather warnings, including rain radar: *bom.gov.au*.

TRAVEL PURSUIT

THE MARCO POLO HOLIDAY QUIZ

Do you know what makes Australia tick? Test your knowledge of the idiosyncrasies and eccentricities of the country and its people. You'll find the answers at the foot of the page, with more detailed explanations on pp18–23.

❶ What are "grey nomads"?
a) Lice that jump from head to head
b) A rare Australian marsupial
c) Retired Australian couples who spend months travelling across the continent in a cosy motorhome

❷ Which category does the platypus belong to?
a) Egg-laying mammal
b) Cloacal reptile
c) Amphibian

❸ Who is Australia's head of state?
a) The Australian Prime Minister
b) The King of the UK
c) The American President

❹ What is the Melbourne Cup?
a) Australia's most prestigious horse race
b) A gourmet competition to find the best coffee
c) Melbourne's biggest football tournament

❺ Which Aussie spider is not poisonous?
a) Huntsman spider
b) Funnel-web spider
c) Redback spider

Answers: 1c, 2a, 3b, 4a, 5a, 6c, 7b, 8c, 9a, 10b

Camping with a view, near Broome

6 What percentage of Australians have at least one parent who was born abroad?
a) 10
b) 25
c) 49

7 What did European geologists find in Kakadu National Park in the early 20th century?
a) Gold
b) Uranium ore
c) Opals

8 What should you do if you are bitten by a potentially poisonous spider?
a) Scream your head off
b) Dab the bite with fresh kangaroo urine
c) Seek medical attention

9 What type of animal is a koala?
a) Marsupial
b) Cuddly toy
c) Bear

10 What does the Royal Flying Doctor Service do?
a) Fly the best Australian doctors to King Charles in Windsor for regular check-ups
b) Provide an emergency medical service to remote Australian regions
c) Send talking drones to accidents

INDEX

Adelaide 9, 144, 153
Adelaide Botanic Garden 145
Adelaide Hills 149
Adelaide River 10, 112
Airlie Beach 95
Alice Springs 117, 171, 179
Alice Springs Desert Park 118
Anglesea 167
Apollo Bay 82, 168
Arnhem Land 116
Art Gallery of New South Wales
   (Sydney) 45
Art Gallery of South Australia
   (Adelaide) 145
Arts Centre Melbourne 80
Atherton Tablelands 102
Australian Museum (Sydney) 8,
   46
Australian National Surfing
   Museum (Torquay) 167
Ayers Rock, see Uluru
Ayers Rock Resort (Yulara) 119,
   173
Baird Bay 151
Balmoral Beach (Sydney) 50
Barossa Valley 2, 149
Batemans Bay 61
Bathurst Island 114
Battery Point (Hobart) 158
Bay of Fires 162
Bay of Martyrs 170
Beauty Point (Tas) 161
beer 28
Bell's Beach 167
Binna Burra 174
Blue Mountains 34, 53
Blue Mountains National Park 2,
   52
Bondi Beach (Sydney) 49
Bowali Visitor Centre 114
Brambuk Aboriginal Cultural
   Centre 84
Brighton 33
Brisbane 90
Broken Hill 66
Bronte Beach (Sydney) 49
Broome 134, 137
Bunbury 132
Bungle Bungle Range 139
Busselton 131
Byron Bay 35, 58
Cable Beach (WA) 135
Cairns 9, 11, 99
Cairns Aquarium 99
Cairns Museum 99
Canberra 63
Cape Byron 58
Cape Leeuwin 131
Cape Le Grand National Park 33
Cape Leveque 136
Cape Naturaliste
   Lighthouse 131
Cape Otway 169
Cape Otway Lighthouse 169
Cape Range National Park 133

Cape Tribulation 105
Cape York 105
Cataract Gorge 160
Central Highlands 30
Central Market (Adelaide) 27
Circular Quay (Sydney) 42, 47
Clare Valley 150
Cleland Wildlife Park
   (Adelaide) 10, 146
coffee 28
Collingwood Children's Farm
   (Melbourne) 10, 79
Coober Pedy 30, 152
Cooloola National Park 94
Coorong National Park 148
Coral Bay (WA) 132
Cradle Mountain 164
Cradle Mountain-Lake St Clair
   National Park 3, 164
Daintree National Park 104, 105
Daintree Rainforest 17
Daintree River 105
Dampier Peninsula 136
Darling Harbour (Sydney) 10,
   46, 47
Darwin 110, 180
Darwin Botanic Gardens 110
Daydream Island 97
Day Dream Silver Mine 68
Deloraine 163
Derby 137, 179
Devonport 163
Dorrigo National Park 60
dreamtime 15, 16, 101, 171
duck-billed platypus 20
Edith Falls 117
Ellery Creek Big Hole 172
Eureka Skydeck (Melbourne) 75
Exmouth 132
Eyre Highway 150
Eyre Peninsula 150
Fairhaven Beach 167
Federation Square
   (Melbourne) 74
Flagstaff Hill Maritime
   Village 170
Flecker Botanic Gardens
   (Cairns) 100
Fleurieu Peninsula 147
Flinders Ranges 33
Flinders Ranges National
   Park 151
Franklin-Gordon Wild Rivers
   National Park 165
Fraser Coast 94
Fraser Island (K'gari) 3, 17, 33,
   94, 105
Fremantle 126
Freycinet National Park 162
Gantheaume Point 135
Geelong 167
Ghan train service 150, 180
Gibb River Road 138
Gibson Steps 169
Glenelg (Adelaide) 146

Gold Coast 35, 93
Gosse-Bluff-Krater 173
Grampians 83, 85
Great Barrier Reef 2, 8, 17, 22,
   32, 86, 96, 97, 98, 99, 101,
   102, 104
Great Dividing Range 60
Great Northern Highway 137,
   139
Great Ocean Road 3, 35, 82, 83,
   166
Great Otway National Park 82,
   168
Hamelin Pool Marine Nature
   Reserve 134
Hamilton Island 97
handicrafts 30
Hastings River 60
Hermannsburg 118
Hervey Bay 94
Hobart 158, 179
Hollybank Treetop
   Adventure 161
Hook Island 97
Hunter Valley 53
Hyams Beach 62
Hyde Park Barracks (Sydney) 45
Immigration Museum
   (Melbourne) 8, 74
Jabiru 114
Jervis Bay National Park 62
Jewel Cave 132
Jim Jim Falls 115
Justice & Police Museum
   (Sydney) 43
Kakadu National Park 2, 11, 18,
   114, 121, 189
Kalgoorlie Boulder 129
Kangaroo Island 3, 148
Kanku Breakaways Conservation
   Park 153
Karijini National Park 134
Kata Tjuta (the Olgas) 119, 120
Katherine 116
Katherine Gorge 116
Katoomba 52
K'gari, see Fraser Island
Kiama 62
Kimberley 137
Kings Canyon (Watarrka) 118,
   121, 173
Kings Cross (Sydney) 47, 51
Kings Park (Perth) 126
koala 189
Koala Hospital (Port
   Macquarie) 9, 60
Koala Sanctuary (Brisbane) 11,
   91
Kununurra 137, 138
Lake St. Clair 164
Lamington National Park 93,
   174
Launceston 160
Lightning Ridge 30

Line of Lode Miners Memorial (Broken Hill) 67
Litchfield National Park 114
Living Desert & Sculptures (Broken Hill) 67
Loch Ard Gorge 169
Logans Beach 170
London Arch 170
Long Island 97
Lorne 169
MacDonnell Ranges 34, 171
Magnetic Island 99
Malcolm Douglas Crocodile Park 136
Manly Beach (Sydney) 50
Margaret River 33, 129
McLaren Vale 147
McPherson Range 93
Melbourne 8, 9, 19, 74, 167, 179, 180
Melbourne Central 80
Melbourne Cup 22, 188
Melbourne Docklands 76, 80, 81
Melbourne Museum 77
Melbourne Star Observation Wheel 76
Melville Island 114
Mereenie Loop Road 173
Migration Museum (Adelaide) 145
Mindil Beach (Darwin) 112
Mission Beach 102
Moana Beach 35
MONA (Hobart) 8, 158
Monkey Mia 134
Mount Kosciuszko 17
Mount Warning National Park 59
Mount Wellington 159
Mungo National Park 69
Murramarang National Park 61
Museum & Art Gallery of the Northern Territory (Darwin) 110
Mutawintji National Park 68
Narooma 69
National Film & Sound Archive (Canberra) 63
National Gallery of Australia (Canberra) 9, 64
National Museum of Australia (Canberra) 64
National Wine Centre (Adelaide) 145
National Wool Museum (Geelong) 167
New South Wales 54
Ngilgi Cave 132
Ninety Mile Beach 17
Ningaloo Reef 32, 132, 133
Nitmiluk National Park 116
Noosa Heads 94
Noosa National Park 94
Noosaville 33
Northern Territory 106
North Stradbroke Island 93

Ochre Pits 172
Old Timers Mine (Coober Pedy) 153
Olgas, see Kata Tjuta
Ormiston Gorge 172
Overland train service 180
Palm Beach 53
Palm Cove 103
Parliament House (Canberra) 65
Perth 126, 178, 179, 180
Perth Mint 126
Phillip Island 81
Pinnacles (Nambung) National Park 128
Port Adelaide 146
Port Arthur 159
Port Augusta 150
Port Campbell 169
Port Campbell National Park 83, 169
Port Douglas 33, 103
Port Fairy 170
Port Macquarie 59
Purnululu National Park 139
Queensland 86
Queensland Cultural Centre (Brisbane) 90
Queenstown 165
Queen Victoria Market (Melbourne) 27, 32, 80
Questacon (Canberra) 10, 65
quokka 128
Redbank Gorge 173
Reef HQ (Townsville) 98
Rocks (Sydney) 44, 50
Rocks Discovery Museum (Sydney) 44
Rottnest Island 128
Royal Botanic Gardens (Melbourne) 76
Royal Botanic Gardens (Sydney) 43
Royal Flying Doctor Service (RFDS) 23, 117, 189
Royal National Park 33, 52
saltwater crocodiles 112
School of the Air (Alice Springs) 117
Sea Acres Rainforest Centre 60
Sealife Aquarium (Melbourne) 75
Sea Life Sydney Aquarium 47
Serpentine Gorge 172
Shrine of Remembrance (Melbourne) 77
Silverton 68
Simpsons Gap 171
Skyrail (Cairns) 100
Snowy Mountains 32, 34
Snowy Mountains National Park 62
South Australia 33, 140
South Australian Museum (Adelaide) 145
South Bank Parklands (Brisbane) 90
South Esk River 160

South Molle 34
South Molle Island 97
spiders 19, 188, 189
Squeaky Beach 83
Standley Chasm 171
Stanley 163
St Helens 162
St Kilda (Melbourne) 33, 77
St Kilda beach 80
Strahan 165
Stuart Highway 150
Sunshine Coast 94
Surfers Paradise 93
Swan Bells (Perth) 126
Sydney 17, 38, 178, 179, 180, 183
Sydney Fish Market 47
Sydney Harbour 34, 42, 43, 53
Sydney Harbour Bridge 42, 44
Sydney Opera House 2, 17, 43, 48, 52
Sydney Tower Eye 46
Tandanya – National Aboriginal Cultural Institute (Adelaide) 145
Taronga Zoo 47
Tasmania 32, 33, 154
Territory Wildlife Park 113
The Three Sisters 52
Tiwi Islands 114
Tjapukai Cultural Centre (Cairns) 100
Torquay 167
Tower Hill State Game Reserve 170
Townsville 98
Twelve Apostles 83, 169
Twelve Apostles Lookout 169
Twin Falls 115
Uluru (Ayers Rock) 8, 119, 173
Uluru-Kata Tjuta National Park 2, 119
uranium 18
Victor Harbor 148
Victoria 70
Warrnambool 170
Watarrka National Park/Kings Canyon 173
Watego's Beach (Byron Bay) 58
Wave Rock 128
Western Australia 122
whale watching 94
White Cliffs 69
Whitsunday Islands 34, 95, 96, 97
Williamstown (Melbourne) 78
Willie Creek Pearl Farm 136
Wilsons Promontory National Park 11, 83, 85
wine 18, 28, 53, 129, 131, 148, 149, 150
Yallingup 34, 131
Yellow River 115
Yulara 120, 173

CREDITS

WE WANT TO HEAR FROM YOU!

Did you have a great holiday? Is there something on your mind? Whatever it is, let us know! Whether you want to praise the guide, alert us to errors or give us a personal tip – MARCO POLO would be pleased to hear from you.

Please contact us by email:

sales@heartwoodpublishing.co.uk

We do everything we can to provide the very latest information for your trip. Nevertheless, despite all of our authors' thorough research, errors can creep in. MARCO POLO does not accept any liability for this.

PICTURE CREDITS
Cover photo: Heart Reef (Huber-images: M. Rellini)
Photos: AWL Images: P. Adams (31), Aurora Photos (186), W. Bibikow (64), M. Bottigelli (140/141), N. Pavitt (Klappe hinten), A. Watson (116); AWL Images/image-broker: G. Zwerger-Schoner (95); AWL Images/John Warburton-Lee: A. Watson (103); DuMont Bildarchiv: Emmler (138/139); Getty Images (158 (Posnov), B. Anupong (78/79), M. Gottschalk (115), J. (161 (Love)), P. S. Kulvong (14/15), D. Osterkamp (70/71); Getty Images/Maremagnum (135); Huber-images: St. Cellai (121), B. Mitchell (58, 113), M. Rellini (46, 92), TC (24/25, 81); laif: C. Emmler (10), G. Theis (176/177); laif/GAMMA-RAPHO: J.-D. Sudres (28); laif/hemis.fr (119, 151); laif/robertharding: R. Harding Production (30/31), M. Runkel (44/45); Look: D. Fuchs (152), P.-A. Hoffmann (6/7); mauritius images: W. Bibikow (11), Boelter (163), I. Boelter (154/155), cgimanufaktur (86/87), R. Linkel (2/3); mauritius images/age fotostock (173); mauritius images/Alamy (8, 23, 49, 129, 166/167), A. Bain (136), R. Ben-Ari (96), M. Gottschalk (68), Imagevixen (122/123), G. Marshall (32/33), H. Maunder (104), A. McComiskey (50), S. Nerrie (147), I. Oeland (54/55), Ch. Putnam (179), W. Robinson (66), St. Sandner (84/85), E. Schlogl (133), P. Scholey (76), A. Scott (162), T. Vyshnya (38/39), D. Wall (111), T. Whitefoot (98); mauritius images/blickwinkel: B. Leitner (106/107); mauritius images/Cavan Images (130); mauritius images/Cultura (26/27); mauritius images/foodcollection (27); mauritius images/fStop: T. Titz (19); mauritius images/imagebroker: K. Petersen (169), N. Probst (34/35), M. Szönyi (cover flaps, 1), M. Weber (100); mauritius images/John Warburton-Lee: A. Watson (63); mauritius images/Loop Images: A. Hare (51); mauritius images/Radius Images (82); mauritius images/robertharding: F. Fell (9), M. Simoni (61); mauritius images/Westend61 (188); C. Melville (191); Okapia/BIOS: Watts (20); T.P. Widmann (149); Shutterstock.com: idiz (12/13), Taras Vyshnya (42), Olga Kashubin (184/185)

3rd Edition – fully revised and updated 2023
Worldwide Distribution: Heartwood Publishing Ltd, Bath, United Kingdom
www.heartwoodpublishing.co.uk

Authors: Esther Blank, Bruni Gebauer, Stefan Huy, Corinna Melville, Urs Wälterlin
Editor: Ulrike Frühwald
Picture editor: Barbara Mehrl
Cartography: © MAIRDUMONT, Ostfildern (pp. 36–37, 168, 172, 175, pull-out map); © MAIRDUMONT, Ostfildern, using data from OpenStreetMap, licence CC-BY-SA 2.0 (pp. 40–41, 52, 56–57, 72–73, 88–89, 91, 108–109, 124–125, 127, 142–143, 144, 156–157)
Cover design and pull-out map cover design: bilekjaeger_Kreativagentur with Zukunftswerkstatt, Stuttgart
Page design: Langenstein Communication GmbH, Ludwigsburg

Heartwood Publishing credits:
Translated from the German by Madeleine Taylor-Laidler, Christopher Wynne and Mo Croasdale
Editors: Felicity Laughton, Kate Michell, Sophie Blacksell Jones
Prepress: Summerlane Books, Bath
Printed in India

MARCO POLO AUTHOR
CORINNA MELVILLE

As a young journalist, Corinna's internship at an Australian newspaper wasn't quite what she expected: instead of egg-laying mammals and deserted islands, she found herself reporting on rather more European events. Nonetheless, her year abroad turned into a lifelong love for the country, which she has called home since 2008. After many years in Melbourne, she now lives with her family in Adelaide.